MODERN POETS
Four

Other Educational Books edited by Jim Hunter

MODERN SHORT STORIES
'The choice of stories is excellent'
The Times Educational Supplement

THE MODERN NOVEL IN ENGLISH:
Studied in Extracts
'an uncommonly good anthology . . . The excerpts
are mostly self-contained episodes and the
accompanying notes are firm and unfussy'
The Times Educational Supplement

Both titles are available in boards and paper covers

Modern Poets
~ FOUR ~

edited by
JIM HUNTER
Senior English Master
Bristol Grammar School

FABER AND FABER
3 Queen Square
London

First published in 1968
by Faber and Faber Limited
3 Queen Square London WC1
Reprinted 1975
Printed in Great Britain by
Whitstable Litho Ltd., Whitstable, Kent

ISBN 0 571 08863 5 (Paper Covers)
ISBN 0 571 08862 7 (hard bound edition)

CONTENTS

9

INTRODUCTION

This book is one of a series of four, which I really see as a single collection. In these four volumes are printed selections from twenty-two modern poets whose language is English. I have tried to pick the poets that it would be most useful to have in such a collection, but it would be rash to assert that these are the best poets of their time. Simpler to say: here are some recent poets that deserve our attention. Choosing them was not easy. The omission I most regret is that of the Scots poet Hugh Mac-Diarmid, a controversial figure but one of the most interesting this century: it was felt that the Lallans in which his best work is written would stand too much in the way of readers of this anthology.

Poets are printed here in order of their date of birth. This seemed sounder than attempting to group them according to patterns which not all readers might accept.

More space has been given to some poets than to others. This should not be seen as crude value-judgement—some poets (e.g. D. H. Lawrence) are more discursive than others (e.g. Wallace Stevens). It is true, of course, that where a poet is given an unusual amount of space this is because he seems to me to offer a wide range of distinguished writing, which should be represented as fairly as possible.

There is still more apparent unfairness in the amount of notes supplied for different poets. But this, too, is not in itself a comment on the merit or interest of the poets:

some modern writers are straightforward, others are difficult. The space for notes in these books has been kept down, in order to print plenty of poetry; and the notes have had to be confined largely to necessary explanation of difficulties, though I have tried to suggest some critical approaches, and have asked one or two questions to keep the reader awake.

In writing the notes I have, of course, drawn freely on various critical works, biographies and commentaries. The notes are intended to be simple and minimal; and anyone seriously studying the poets will need to read about their work and lives for himself. In choosing poets and poems, and in writing the notes, I have been helped by conversation with a number of friends, and in particular by Frank Beecroft, Bill Haxworth, Fred Inglis, and Andor Gomme.

Philip Larkin

Philip Larkin was born in 1922 and brought up in Coventry. He was educated at Oxford, and since then has had various posts as a librarian. He is now librarian of the University of Hull. He has published three books of poetry and two novels.

Larkin is one of the most popular poets of today, for his clarity and honesty. He is an extreme version of the 1950's anti-hero: visiting a church he doesn't even give a valid sixpence, he is sardonic at the expense (as it seems) of religious faith, marriage, family and (by implication) of literary pretension also, for he writes in a prosaic colloquial manner and is never obscure. His subject-matter is faceless urban civilization and a faceless middle-class world: a world of defeat, tawdriness and suppressed or underdeveloped emotions. The odd thing is that he seems to relish all this, rather as the even more popular John Betjeman relishes the world of the *Daily Telegraph* reader.

But Larkin's relish is something subtler and more positive than that of Betjeman, I think: beneath his irony lies a considerable respect for many of the things he affects to deride (the conclusions of CHURCH-GOING and THE WHITSUN WEDDINGS show this clearly enough); and these include traditional poetic nobility. Larkin's poetry tends constantly, beneath its flatness and colloquialism, towards the classic pentameter line:

> A serious house on serious earth it is
> In whose blent air all our compulsions meet
> Are recognized, and robed as destinies . . .
>
> CHURCH-GOING

or the conventions of poetic music:

> Brings closer what is left to come,
> And dulls to distance all we are.
>
> AMBULANCES

Technically there is much to admire in Larkin: the deceptive ease of his lines and rhymes, the delicate variety of verse-movement, and its very English understatement. And a number of his poems express particularly clearly and decently intellectual attitudes important to our times. CHURCH-GOING, for example, is a poem many readers will turn to with relief for its expression of their ambiguous agnosticism, an expression much clearer than they could formulate themselves. And FAITH-HEALING expresses, with a distinguished combination of penetration and good taste, feelings which in most of us remain those of confused embarrassment or uneasiness.

Poem XVI from *The North Ship*

The bottle is drunk out by one;
At two, the book is shut;
At three, the lovers lie apart,
Love and its commerce done;
And now the luminous watch-hands
Show after four-o'clock,
Time of night when straying winds
Trouble the dark.

And I am sick for want of sleep;
So sick, that I can half-believe
The soundless river pouring from the cave
Is neither strong, nor deep;
Only an image fancied in conceit.
I lie and wait for morning, and the birds,
The first steps going down the unswept street,
Voices of girls with scarfs around their heads.

Wedding-Wind

The wind blew all my wedding-day,
And my wedding-night was the night of the high wind;
And a stable door was banging, again and again,
That he must go and shut it, leaving me
Stupid in candlelight, hearing rain,
Seeing my face in the twisted candlestick,
Yet seeing nothing. When he came back
He said the horses were restless, and I was sad
That any man or beast that night should lack
The happiness I had.

Now in the day
All's ravelled under the sun by the wind's blowing.
He has gone to look at the floods, and I
Carry a chipped pail to the chicken-run,
Set it down, and stare. All is the wind
Hunting through clouds and forests, thrashing
My apron and the hanging cloths on the line.
Can it be borne, this bodying-forth by wind
Of joy my actions turn on, like a thread
Carrying beads? Shall I be let to sleep
Now this perpetual morning shares my bed?
Can even death dry up
These new delighted lakes, conclude
Our kneeling as cattle by all-generous waters?

Church-Going

Once I am sure there's nothing going on'
I step inside, letting the door thud shut.
Another church: matting, seats, and stone,
And little books; sprawlings of flowers, cut
For Sunday, brownish now; some brass and stuff
Up at the holy end; the small neat organ;
And a tense, musty, unignorable silence,
Brewed God knows how long. Hatless, I take off
My cycle-clips in awkward reverence,

*Short mono syllabic words prod
sense of harshness, violence*

Move forward, run my hand around the font.
From where I stand, the roof looks almost new—
Cleaned, or restored? Someone would know: I don't.
Mounting the lectern, I peruse a few
Hectoring large-scale verses, and pronounce
'Here endeth' much more loudly than I'd meant.
The echoes snigger briefly. Back at the door
I sign the book, donate an Irish sixpence,
Reflect the place was not worth stopping for.

*Onomatopoeia often by alliteration &
sharp harsh sounds prod a similar effect*

Yet stop I did: in fact I often do,   *"fierce fuse"*
And always end much at a loss like this,
Wondering what to look for; wondering, too,
When churches fall completely out of use
What we shall turn them into, if we shall keep
A few cathedrals chronically on show,
Their parchment, plate, and pyx in locked cases,
And let the rest rent-free to rain and sheep.
Shall we avoid them ás unlucky places?

rhy conf w & ideas to set pat.

Or, after dark, will dubious women come
To make their children touch a particular stone;
Pick simples for a cancer; or on some
Advised night see walking a dead one?
Power of some sort or other will go on
In games, in riddles, seemingly at random;
But superstition, like belief, must die,
And what remains when disbelief has gone?
Grass, weedy pavement, brambles, buttress, sky,

A shape less recognizable each week,
A purpose more obscure. I wonder who
Will be the last, the very last, to seek
This place for what it was; one of the crew
That tap and jot and know what roodlofts were?
Some ruin-bibber, randy for antique,
Or Christmas-addict, counting on a whiff
Of gown-and-bands and organ-pipes and myrrh?
Or will he be my representative,

Bored, uninformed, knowing the ghostly silt
Dispersed, yet tending to this cross of ground
Through suburb scrub because it held unspilt
So long and equably what since is found
Only in separation—marriage, and birth,
And death, and thoughts of these—for which was built
This special shell? For, though I've no idea
What this accoutred frowsty barn is worth,
It pleases me to stand in silence here;

A serious house on serious earth it is,
In whose blent air all our compulsions meet,
Are recognized, and robed as destinies.

18

And that much never will be obsolete,
Since someone will for ever be surprising
A hunger in himself to be more serious,
And gravitating with it to this ground,
Which, he once heard, was proper to grow wise in,
If only that so many dead lie round.

Faith-Healing

Slowly the women file to where he stands
Upright in rimless glasses, silver hair,
Dark suit, white collar. Stewards tirelessly
Persuade them onwards to his voice and hands,
Within whose warm spring rain of loving care
Each dwells some twenty seconds. *Now, dear child,
What's wrong*, the deep American voice demands,
And, scarcely pausing, goes into a prayer
Directing God about this eye, that knee.
Their heads are clasped abruptly; then, exiled

Like losing thoughts, they go in silence; some
Sheepishly stray, not back into their lives
Just yet; but some stay stiff, twitching and loud
With deep hoarse tears, as if a kind of dumb
And idiot child within them still survives
To re-awake at kindness, thinking a voice
At last calls them alone, that hands have come
To lift and lighten; and such joy arrives
Their thick tongues blort, their eyes squeeze grief, a crowd
Of huge unheard answers jam and rejoice—

What's wrong! Moustached in flowered frocks they shake:
By now, all's wrong. In everyone there sleeps
A sense of life lived according to love.
To some it means the difference they could make
By loving others, but across most it sweeps
As all they might have done had they been loved.
That nothing cures. An immense slackening ache,
As when, thawing, the rigid landscape weeps,
Spreads slowly through them—that, and the voice above
Saying *Dear child*, and all time has disproved.

The Whitsun Weddings

That Whitsun, I was late getting away:
    Not till about
One-twenty on the sunlit Saturday
Did my three-quarters-empty train pull out,
All windows down, all cushions hot, all sense
Of being in a hurry gone. We ran
Behind the backs of houses, crossed a street
Of blinding windscreens, smelt the fish-docks thence
The river's level drifting breadth began,
Where sky and Lincolnshire and water meet.

All afternoon, through the tall heat that slept
    For miles inland,
A slow and stopping curve southwards we kept.
Wide farms went by, short-shadowed cattle, and
Canals with floatings of industrial froth;
A hothouse flashed, uniquely; hedges dipped
And rose; and now and then a smell of grass
Displaced the reek of buttoned carriage-cloth
Until the next town, new and nondescript,
Approached with acres of dismantled cars.

At first, I didn't notice what a noise
    The weddings made
Each station that we stopped at: sun destroys
The interest of what's happening in the shade,
And down the long cool platforms whoops and skirls
I took for porters larking with the mails
And went on reading. Once we started, though,
We passed them, grinning and pomaded, girls
In parodies of fashion, heels and veils,
All posed irresolutely, watching us go,

As if out on the end of an event
    Waving good-bye
To something that survived it. Struck, I leant
More promptly out next time, more curiously,
And saw it all again in different terms:
The fathers with broad belts under their suits
And seamy foreheads: mothers loud and fat;
An uncle shouting smut; and then the perms,
The nylon gloves and jewellery-substitutes,
The meons, mauves, and olive-ochres that

Marked off the girls unreally from the rest.
    Yes, from cafés
And banquet-halls up yards, and bunting-dressed
Coach-party annexes, the wedding-days
Were coming to an end. All down the line
Fresh couples climbed aboard; the rest stood round;
The last confetti and advice were thrown,
And, as we moved, each face seemed to define
Just what it saw departing: children frowned
At something dull; fathers had never known

Success so huge and wholly farcical;
    The women shared
The secret like a happy funeral;
While girls, gripping their handbags tighter, stared
At a religious wounding. Free at last,
And loaded with the sum of all they saw,
We hurried towards London, shuffling gouts of steam.
Now fields were building-plots, and poplars cast
Long shadows over major roads, and for
Some fifty minutes, that in time would seem

Just long enough to settle hats and say
  I nearly died
A dozen marriages got under way.
They watched the landscape, sitting side by side
—An Odeon went past, a cooling tower,
And someone running up to bowl—and none
Thought of the others they would never meet
Or how their lives would all contain this hour.
I thought of London spread out in the sun,
In postal districts packed like squares of wheat:

There we were aimed. And as we raced across
  Bright knots of rail
Past standing Pullmans, walls of blackened moss
Came close, and it was nearly done, this frail
Travelling coincidence; and what it held
Stood ready to be loosed with all the power
That being changed can give. We slowed again,
And as the tightened brakes took hold, there swelled
A sense of falling, like an arrow-shower
Sent out of sight, somewhere becoming rain.

MCMXIV

Those long uneven lines
Standing as patiently
As if they were stretched outside
The Oval or Villa Park,
The crowns of hats, the sun
On moustached archaic faces
Grinning as if it were all
An August Bank Holiday lark;

And the shut shops, the bleached
Established names on the sunblinds,
The farthings and the sovereigns,
And dark-clothed children at play
Called after kings and queens,
The tin advertisements
For cocoa and twist, and the pubs
Wide open all day;

And the countryside not caring:
The place-names all hazed over
With flowering grasses, and fields
Shadowing Doomsday lines
Under wheat's restless silence;
The differently-dressed servants
With tiny rooms in huge houses,
The dust behind limousines;

Never such innocence,
Never before or since,
As changed itself to past
Without a word—the men
Leaving the gardens tidy,
The thousands of marriages
Lasting a little while longer:
Never such innocence again.

Ambulances

Closed like confessionals, they thread
Loud noons of cities, giving back
None of the glances they absorb.
Light glossy grey, arms on a plaque,
They come to rest at any kerb:
All streets in time are visited.

Then children strewn on steps or road,
Or women coming from the shops
Past smells of different dinners, see
A wild white face that overtops
Red stretcher-blankets momently
As it is carried in and stowed,

And sense the solving emptiness
That lies just under all we do,
And for a second get it whole,
So permanent and blank and true,
The fastened doors recede. *Poor soul*,
They whisper at their own distress;

25

atmosphere of death

For borne away in deadened air

death as May go the sudden shut of loss *seperation*

Round something nearly at an end,

And what cohered in it across

tran persons normal The years, the unique random blend *habits exp*

Of families and fashions, there *& relat.*

behaviour

emph. pat
cut off family At last begin to loosen. Far
as death appr. From the exchange of love to lie

Unreachable inside a room

The traffic parts to let go by

Brings closer what is left to come, *implies nothing*

And dulls to distance all we are. *but sep.*

Frequ. use of allit. – which perh. sug
the "slow emp" – grad slip away into d.
& nothingness

½ rhymes – insecurity

Dockery and Son

'Dockery was junior to you,
Wasn't he?' said the Dean. 'His son's here now.'
Death-suited, visitant, I nod. 'And do
You keep in touch with—' Or remember how
Black-gowned, unbreakfasted, and still half-tight
We used to stand before that desk, to give
'Our version' of 'these incidents last night'?
I try the door of where I used to live:

Locked. The lawn spreads dazzlingly wide.
A known bell chimes. I catch my train, ignored.
Canal and clouds and colleges subside
Slowly from view. But Dockery, good Lord,
Anyone up today must have been born
In '43, when I was twenty-one.
If he was younger, did he get this son
At nineteen, twenty? Was he that withdrawn

High-collared public-schoolboy, sharing rooms
With Cartwright who was killed? Well, it just shows
How much . . . How little. . . . Yawning, I suppose
I fell asleep, waking at the fumes
And furnace-glares of Sheffield, where I changed,
And ate an awful pie, and walked along
The platform to its end to see the ranged
Joining and parting lines reflect a strong

Unhindered moon. To have no son, no wife,
No house or land still seemed quite natural.
Only a numbness registered the shock
Of finding out how much had gone of life,

How widely from the others. Dockery, now:
Only nineteen, he must have taken stock
Of what he wanted, and been capable
Of . . . No, that's not the difference: rather, how

Convinced he was he should be added to!
Why did he think adding meant increase?
To me it was dilution. Where do these
Innate assumptions come from? Not from what
We think truest, or most want to do:
Those warp tight-shut, like doors. They're more a style
Our lives bring with them: habit for a while,
Suddenly they harden into all we've got

And how we got it; looked back on, they rear
Like sand-clouds, thick and close, embodying
For Dockery a son, for me nothing,
Nothing with all a son's harsh patronage.
Life is first boredom, then fear.
Whether or not we use it, it goes,
And leaves what something hidden from us chose,
And age, and then the only end of age.

Afternoons

Summer is fading:
The leaves fall in ones and twos
From trees bordering
The new recreation ground.
In the hollows of afternoons
Young mothers assemble
At swing and sandpit
Setting free their children.

Behind them, at intervals,
Stand husbands in skilled trades,
An estateful of washing,
And the albums, lettered
Our Wedding, lying
Near the television:
Before them, the wind
Is ruining their courting-places

That are still courting-places
(But the lovers are all in school),
And their children, so intent on
Finding more unripe acorns,
Expect to be taken home.
Their beauty has thickened.
Something is pushing them
To the side of their own lives.

Notes

POEM XVI from *The North Ship*

The North Ship was Larkin's first book, a collection of love-lyrics. This poem is a masterpiece of controlled verse-movement and rhyme-sound: what might have been flabby is made both brisk and haunting.

WEDDING-WIND

The poet writes in the person of a girl newly married to a farmer; and brings to this Browningesque framework a freer lyricism and more energetic verse than he usually permits himself. There is perhaps cause for regret that Larkin has not pursued this fictional, imaginative line: possibly he feels it to be self-indulgent and falsely 'literary', though there seems to me to be nothing false about this stable door or this chipped pail.

Note again the music of the verse, the varied placing of the caesuras. It is a poem that asks to be spoken aloud.

CHURCH-GOING

pyx: vessel in which consecrated bread is kept.
simples: medicinal herbs.
accoutred: cluttered.
blent: blended. See the previous verse: *because it held*
So long and equably what since is found
Only in separation . . .

THE WHITSUN WEDDINGS

Larkin shares with some modern novelists a gift for capturing humdrum reality vividly on the page. The poet here is not an august literary personage on a different plane from ourselves: on the contrary, supposing we travelled south from Hull one Whit Saturday a few years ago, we were perhaps in the same compartment with him. The windscreens, the industrial froth, the man running up to bowl, the *major* in 'the poplars cast Long shadows over major roads': these make the back-ground of the poem real, and the foreground (the weddings) has the more urgency. It might even have been our wedding!

The ease of Larkin's style should not tempt us to skim the thought of the poem, which is of considerable delicacy and subtlety. A less ambitious poem of similar purport is Seamus Heaney's HONEYMOON FLIGHT: it may be helpful to compare the two.

MCMXIV

The poet has been looking at photographs of 1914—men queuing up to enlist in the war. The last verse is not frivolous: its idea is one many commentators would endorse—that those days of 1914, before the real scale and nature of world war had been realized, were the last of this illusion and innocence.

AMBULANCES

In modern urban life we tend to forget about death. The shock of seeing the ambulance restores a true scale of values to us; 'for a second' we 'get it whole': our death seems real to us again, our present lives almost irrelevant.

DOCKERY AND SON

The poet has been revisiting his Oxford college for a funeral.

This is a poem of disconcerting, humbling frankness, though few readers may share the uncompromising negative-ness of Larkin's outlook.

AFTERNOONS

The poet may (remembering DOCKERY AND SON) be accused here of calling the grapes sour. Yet I think the poem does offer a valid warning about one aspect of British society in recent years: the tendency to marry young and have children young, after which—perhaps before people are thirty—life seems to offer very little else. Love today, the poet suggests, is reckoned to be a thing of one's teens ('the lovers are all in school'). The reference to 'unripe acorns' is not accidental.

Louis Simpson

Louis Simpson was born in Jamaica in 1923, and has lived in America since 1940. He spent three years in the United States Army during the Second World War; and since then has been a publisher and a university teacher. His first book of poetry was published in 1949, and he now has a considerable reputation in America, though comparatively little known over here.

Simpson to me represents much of the best about modern American literature. American writing is now rarely either consciously indebted or consciously hostile to European models: it has its own character and its own voices. One of its most remarkable achievements, I think, is a rediscovery of simplicity: that apparent naivety of diction and thought which is best known in the prose of Ernest Hemingway. American poetry since the war excels in terseness and in clarity of word and image—though, as has always been the case, the simplest writing is often the most difficult to paraphrase or explain, and the 'meaning' of a poem of clear images may be anything but clear.

One reason for this is a concentration upon the *material* of experience, not its significance. The things and happenings are not explicitly interpreted: the writer's attitude towards them must be gathered from the terms and form in which he describes them. Another reason is a presumably conscious return to the basic vocabulary of colloquial speech: simple words are redeemed by being used delicately and in brief statements—clearly they would be weak in a poem that gushed. Again, if you know Hemingway you will know what I mean; and also, perhaps, if you know the poetry of William Carlos Williams, who has probably influenced many young American poets.

Together with this clarity of word and concreteness of image often goes, however, quite unfamiliar association of word and image, and cryptic half-mystical statements, to which we may respond but which it is very difficult to discuss. One can say very little, I feel, about Simpson's poems LOVE, MY MACHINE or WIND, CLOUDS, AND THE DELICATE CURVE OF THE WORLD, though they seem to me to be genuine explorations of a promising kind.

Simpson is generally a sombre poet, depressed by that aspect of human kind which emerged in Nazi persecutors, by the futility of war itself, and by the falsehood and weariness he senses in the United States today. On the other hand there is a resilience in him which leads him at the least to a spirited irony, and sometimes to search, with a suggestion of hope, for some transcendental experience ('I am going into the night to find a world of my own'). He seems to me to express particularly sharply some aspects of Western feeling in the third quarter of the twentieth century; and, besides that, to be in a minor but important way a renovator of poetic language and verse.

As Birds are Fitted to the Boughs

As birds are fitted to the boughs
That blossom on the tree
And whisper when the south wind blows—
So was my love to me.

And still she blossoms in my mind
And whispers softly, though
The clouds are fitted to the wind,
The wind is to the snow.

Old Soldier

A dream of battle on a windy night
Has wakened him. The shadows move once more
With rumours of alarm. He sees the height
And helmet of his terror in the door.

The guns reverberate; a livid arc
From sky to sky lightens the windowpanes
And all his room. The clock ticks in the dark;
A cool wind stirs the curtains, and it rains.

He lies remembering: 'That's how it was . . .'
And smiles, and drifts into a youthful sleep
Without a care. His life is all he has,
And that is given to the guards to keep.

The Battle

Helmet and rifle, pack and overcoat
Marched through a forest. Somewhere up ahead
Guns thudded. Like the circle of a throat
The night on every side was turning red.

They halted and they dug. They sank like moles
Into the clammy earth between the trees.
And soon the sentries, standing in their holes,
Felt the first snow. Their feet began to freeze.

At dawn the first shell landed with a crack.
Then shells and bullets swept the icy woods.
This lasted many days. The snow was black.
The corpses stiffened in their scarlet hoods.

Most clearly of that battle I remember
The tiredness in eyes, how hands looked thin
Around a cigarette, and the bright ember
Would pulse with all the life there was within.

Memories of a Lost War

The guns know what is what, but underneath
In fearful file
We go around burst boots and packs and teeth
That seem to smile.

The scene jags like a strip of celluloid,
A mortar fires,
Cinzano falls, Michelin is destroyed,
The man of tires.

As darkness drifts like fog in from the sea
Somebody says
'We're digging in.' Look well, for this may be
The last of days.

Hot lightnings stitch the blind eye of the moon,
The thunder's blunt.
We sleep. Our dreams pass in a faint platoon
Towards the front.

Sleep well, for you are young. Each tree and bush
Drips with sweet dew,
And earlier than morning June's cool hush
Will waken you.

The riflemen will wake and hold their breath.
Though they may bleed
They will be proud a while of something death
Still seems to need.

Hot Night on Water Street

A hot midsummer night on Water Street—
The boys in jeans were combing their blond hair,
Watching the girls go by on tired feet;
And an old woman with a witch's stare
Cried 'Praise the Lord!' She vanished on a bus
With hissing air brakes, like an incubus.

Three hardware stores, a barbershop, a bar,
A movie playing Westerns—where I went
To see a dream of horses called The Star. . . .
Some day, when this uncertain continent
Is marble, and men ask what was the good
We lived by, dust may whisper 'Hollywood.'

Then back along the river bank on foot
By moonlight. . . . On the West Virginia side
An owlish train began to huff and hoot;
It seemed to know of something that had died.
I didn't linger—sometimes when I travel
I think I'm being followed by the Devil.

At the newsstand in the lobby, a cigar
Was talkative: 'Since I've been in this town
I've seen one likely woman, and a car
As she was crossing Main Street knocked her down.'
I was a stranger here myself, I said,
And bought the New York Times, and went to bed.

The Silent Generation

When Hitler was the Devil
He did as he had sworn
With such enthusiasm
That even, donnerwetter,
The Germans say, 'Far better
Had he been never born!'

It was my generation
That put the Devil down
With great enthusiasm.
But now our occupation
Is gone. Our education
Is wasted on the town.

We lack enthusiasm.
Life seems a mystery;
It's like the play a lady
Told me about: 'it's not . . .
It doesn't have a plot,'
She said, 'it's history.'

The Goodnight

He stood still by her bed
Watching his daughter breathe,
The dark and silver head,
The fingers curled beneath,
And thought: Though she may have
Intelligence and charm
And luck, they will not save
Her life from every harm.

The lives of children are
Dangerous to their parents
With fire, water, air,
And other accidents;
And some for a child's sake,
Anticipating doom,
Empty the world to make
The world safe as a room.

Who could endure the pain
That was Laocoön's?
Twisting, he saw again
In the same coil his sons.
Plumed in his father's skill,
Young Icarus flew higher
Towards the sun, until
He fell in rings of fire.

A man who cannot stand
Children's perilous play,
With lifted voice and hand
Drives the children away.

Out of sight, out of reach,
The tumbling children pass;
He sits on an empty beach,
Holding an empty glass.

Who said that tenderness
Will turn the heart to stone?
May I endure her weakness
As I endure my own.
Better to say goodnight
To breathing flesh and blood
Each night as though the night
Were always only good.

A Story about Chicken Soup

In my grandmother's house there was always chicken
        soup
And talk of the old country—mud and boards,
Poverty,
The snow falling down the necks of lovers.

Now and then, out of her savings
She sent them a dowry. Imagine
The rice-powdered faces!
And the smell of the bride, like chicken soup.

But the Germans killed them.
I know it's in bad taste to say it,
But it's true. The Germans killed them all.

*

In the ruins of Berchtesgaden
A child with yellow hair
Ran out of a doorway.

A German girl-child—
Cuckoo, all skin and bones—
Not even enough to make chicken soup.
She sat by the stream and smiled.
Then as we splashed in the sun
She laughed at us.
We had killed her mechanical brothers,
So we forgave her.

*

The sun is shining.
The shadows of the lovers have disappeared.
They are all eyes; they have some demand on me—
They want me to be more serious than I want to be.

They want me to stick in their mudhole
Where no one is elegant.
They want me to wear old clothes,
They want me to be poor, to sleep in a room with many
        others—

Not to walk in the painted sunshine
To a summer house,
But to live in the tragic world forever.

On the Lawn at the Villa

On the lawn at the villa—
That's the way to start, eh, reader?
We know where we stand—somewhere expensive—
You and I *imperturbes*, as Walt would say,
Before the diversions of wealth, you and I *engagés*.

On the lawn at the villa
Sat a manufacturer of explosives,
His wife from Paris,
And a young man named Bruno,

And myself, being American,
Willing to talk to these malefactors,
The manufacturer of explosives, and so on,
But somehow superior. By that I mean democratic.
It's complicated, being an American,
Having the money and the bad conscience, both at the
        same time.
Perhaps, after all, this is not the right subject for a poem.

We were all sitting there paralysed
In the hot Tuscan afternoon,
And the bodies of the machine-gun crew were draped
        over the balcony.
So we sat there all afternoon.

Love, My Machine

Love, my machine,
We rise by this escape,
We travel on the shocks we make.

For every man and woman
Is an immortal spirit
Trapped and dazed on a star shoot.

Tokyo, come in!
Yuzuru Karagiri, do you read me?
San Francisco, darkest of cities, do you read me?

Here is eternal space,
Here is eternal solitude.
Is it any different with you on earth?

There are so many here!
Here's Gandhi, here's Jesus,
Moses, and all the other practical people.

By the light of the stars
This night is serious.
I am going into the night to find a world of my own.

Wind, Clouds, and the Delicate Curve of the World

Wind, clouds, and the delicate curve of the world
Stretching so far away . . .
On a cloud in the clear sight of heaven
Sit Kali and Jesus, disputing.
Tree shadows, cloud shadows
Falling across the body of the world
That sleeps with one arm thrown across her eyes . . .
A wind stirs in the daisies
And trees are sighing,
'These houses and these gardens are illusions.'
Leaf shadows, cloud shadows,
And the wind moving as far as the eye can reach . . .

Walt Whitman at Bear Mountain

*. . . life which does not give the preference to any other life, of any previous
period, which therefore prefers its own existence . . .*
ORTEGA Y GASSET

Neither on horseback nor seated,
But like himself, squarely on two feet,
The poet of death and lilacs
Loafs by the footpath. Even the bronze looks alive
Where it is folded like cloth. And he seems friendly.

'Where is the Mississippi panorama
And the girl who played the piano?
Where are you, Walt?
The Open Road goes to the used-car lot.

'Where is the nation you promised?
These houses built of wood sustain
Colossal snows,
And the light above the street is sick to death.

'As for the people—see how they neglect you!
Only a poet pauses to read the inscription.'

'I am here,' he answered.
'It seems you have found me out.
Yet, did I not warn you that it was Myself
I advertised? Were my words not sufficiently plain?

'I gave no prescriptions,
And those who have taken my moods for prophecies
Mistake the matter.'
Then, vastly amused—'Why do you reproach me?
I freely confess I am wholly disreputable.
Yet I am happy, because you have found me out.'

A crocodile in wrinkled metal loafing . . .

Then all the realtors,
Pickpockets, salesmen, and the actors performing
Official scenarios,
Turned a deaf ear, for they had contracted
American dreams.

But the man who keeps a store on a lonely road,
And the housewife who knows she's dumb,
And the earth, are relieved.

All that grave weight of America
Cancelled! Like Greece and Rome.
The future in ruins!
The castles, the prisons, the cathedrals
Unbuilding, and roses
Blossoming from the stones that are not there . . .

The clouds are lifting from the high Sierras,
The Bay mists clearing.
And the angel in the gate, the flowering plum,
Dances like Italy, imagining red.

American Classic

It's a classic American scene—
A car stopped off the road
And a man trying to repair it.

The woman who stays in the car
In the classic American scene
Stares back at the freeway traffic.

They look surprised, and ashamed
To be so helpless . . .
Let down in the middle of the road!

To think that their car would do this!
They look like mountain people
Whose son has gone against the law.

But every night they set out food
And the robber goes skulking back to the trees.
That's how it is with the car . . .

It's theirs. They're stuck with it.
Now they know what it's like to sit
And see the world go whizzing by.

In the fume of carbon monoxide and dust
They are not such good Americans
As they thought they were.

The feeling of being left out
Through no fault of your own,
                              is common.
That's why I say, an American classic.

After Midnight

The dark streets are deserted,
With only a drugstore glowing
Softly, like a sleeping body;

With one white, naked bulb
In the back, that shines
On suicides and abortions.

Who lives in these dark houses?
I am suddenly aware
I might live here myself.

The garage man returns
And puts the change in my hand,
Counting the singles carefully.

Notes

AS BIRDS ARE FITTED TO THE BOUGHS

The significance of this poem is that it appeared in the 1950's. In isolation it might suggest merely an escapist academic retreating to the past: in the context of Simpson's other work it shows an earnest concern for clear musical expression, a reaction against twentieth-century looseness and discursiveness, as well as the obvious interest in literary and popular tradition.

THE BATTLE

More understatement. The expression is lumpish and heavy, with a weariness identified in the last verse. The placing of pauses within the lines, and the firm simplicity of the diction, are not accidental.

MEMORIES OF A LOST WAR

A poem of the tersest expression, but packed with descriptive detail and poignancy; it compares interestingly with Wilfred Owen's trench-poems of 1918.

The second verse refers to the advertisements painted on walls which are being destroyed. 'The man of tires' is a Michelin advertisement familiar in Europe. The previous line suggests that Cinzano and Michelin are notable military targets: the man of tires is an anti-climax.

Falcons' eyes used to be stitched up; the image is probably used here for its suggestion of fierce pain, and perhaps for the darting effect of lightning, like a modern sewing machine. 'Blunt' is economical and effective onomatopoeia.

I think the last lines mean that even in modern warfare death still needs courage, or a sense of self-sacrifice, or simply dignity.

49

HOT NIGHT ON WATER STREET

A comment on the 'uncertain continent' of America, where the cry of 'Praise the Lord!' seems that of a nightmarish evil spirit, and where the train seems 'to know of something that had died' and the poet feels himself a stranger.

THE GOODNIGHT

We cannot over-protect our children: they must necessarily be exposed to dangers as we are, and will be endangered by their own weakness as we are. These are essential conditions of being fully alive. One must live in trust rather than in constant suspicion and fear. The poem is a sort of modern agnostic prayer or hymn, with a simple delicacy one is glad to see in modern poetry.

A STORY ABOUT CHICKEN SOUP

dowry: a gift to a couple getting married (originally it was a sum of money paid to the husband by the bride's father). The rice was thrown at the weddings.

Berchtesgaden: the country home of Adolf Hitler. The place has a special significance for Louis Simpson, who received his American citizenship there.

Is it ever possible, the poem asks, to be gay and happy again, without guilt at the memory of those exterminated by Nazism? It seems we owe them our perpetual mourning: that seems the least (and, in a way, all) we can do. Yet human emotions do not and cannot work so loyally and unselfishly; and life today has sunlight in it. So the poet lives in a half-guilt, returning at intervals to the fact of that hideous slaughter, whether it is 'in bad taste' to mention it or not.

ON THE LAWN AT THE VILLA

Walt: Walt Whitman, who often addresses the reader personally, and who uses the phrase *imperturbe*, which I take to mean 'imperturbable'.

Engagés: literally 'committed'—perhaps here sardonic: 'we liberals . . .'.

This is an anti-poem: the poet breaks off at the very outset to deride himself; and later his disgust becomes overwhelming:

'Perhaps, after all, this is not the right subject for a poem.' He is disgusted by his own readiness 'to talk to these malefactors'—picturing in his mind 'the bodies of the machine-gun crew . . . draped over the balcony'—but also by his own tendency to feel morally superior to the manufacturer of explosives, while enjoying himself the capitalist society which depends partly upon such manufacturers. A poem of confession and defeat: but at least an honest one.

LOVE, MY MACHINE
'Come in' and 'do you read me' are terms used by radio operators (especially in flying; compare the first three lines, where love seems to be seen as a flying machine).

WIND, CLOUDS, AND THE DELICATE CURVE OF THE WORLD
Kali: goddess of death and destruction in Hindu mythology.

WALT WHITMAN AT BEAR MOUNTAIN
The poet is looking at a statue of Whitman, who in the mid-nineteenth century spoke extravagantly of the moral and spiritual grandeur of America. These supposed prophecies have a sad look today; but some modern Americans, especially those whose work leads them into automatic falsification, keep them alive. Whitman, however, didn't mean to load such artificial responsibilities on to the future; he was really celebrating himself, his own exultation in life, not his country. The best of America, says Simpson, is when she forgets her Whitmanesque preconceived ideals and lives her own life spontaneously and naturally. Then the clouds lift and the spirit is freed.

3. Refers to Whitman's many fine poems on death, and in particular to his elegy for Abraham Lincoln, *When Lilacs Last in the Dooryard Bloomed*.

9. *the Open Road*: Whitman invited his reader to join him, journeying at random through America and through life.

AFTER MIDNIGHT

Almost like an Imagist poem of Ezra Pound or his followers in the 1920's: which means that it is also rather like oriental poetry. (There is something of the same quality in LOVE, MY MACHINE and WIND, CLOUDS, AND THE DELICATE CURVE OF THE WORLD.) The images and mood are not interpreted: they are naked for the reader and startle him. The verse is delicately poised: the whole poem a skilful example of suggestion and understatement.

Charles Tomlinson

Charles Tomlinson was born at Stoke-on-Trent in 1927: he read English at Cambridge, and was a schoolteacher and a private secretary before becoming a university teacher. He is now lecturer in English at the University of Bristol, and he has also taught in New Mexico. His first book of poetry, *The Necklace*, was published in 1955; since then he has published several further volumes, including translations.

Tomlinson's reputation has grown quietly, but will probably outlast many more suddenly gained. He is unrepentantly a highbrow, a poet of relatively severe intellectual precision amongst much post-war violence and loose emotion. The tone of his work is cool and meticulous, with a disdain for cheap effects and a deep respect for language. One imagines that Ezra Pound is a poet he admires, and perhaps T. S. Eliot; while his later work, tending to terser expression and less abstract comment, shows considerable awareness of modern American poetry.

Tomlinson is probably the best of a number of recent poets who are returning—by both personal inclination and literary conviction—to an 'aesthetic' view of poetry. This aestheticism is well removed from the fatuous excesses of the late nineteenth century, but it has a good deal in common with one of the pioneers of nineteenth-century aestheticism, Théophile Gautier, and with the twentieth-century pioneers Ezra Pound and Wallace Stevens. The poem is a work of art, of making and shaping: its excellence is *as a poem*, not as a piece of propaganda or philosophy, and its subject-matter is life as emotional and sensuous experience—which (it is implied) need not be shallow or limited. Poems such as WHAT IT WAS LIKE and HOW IT HAPPENED may help to illustrate this.

This view of poetry is often linked with a sense of kinship

with other arts (rather than with, say, politics or religion); in Tomlinson's case there is a close association with painting or drawing. He excels at visual description, and quite explicitly at times comments on the formal composition of the scene he is describing (e.g. in verse three of ON THE HALL AT STOWEY).

Ideas, however, are by no means excluded from such poetry: Tomlinson's poems are full of solid matter for the intellect, more or less paraphrasable. But (he might say) this is the matter of poetry, of the artefact, and not something else in disguise. He stands far removed from the 'committed' poets of the 1930's, and would feel no need to apologize for that. He is reasserting the art of poetry, and this may be a surer way of helping poetry to continue and develop than a self-conscious search for topicality.

The Atlantic

Launched into an opposing wind, hangs
Grappled beneath the onrush,
And there, lifts, curling in spume,
Unlocks, drops from that hold
Over and shoreward. The beach receives it,
A whitening line, collapsing
Powdering-off down its broken length;
Then, curded, shallow, heavy
With clustering bubbles, it nears
In a slow sheet that must climb
Relinquishing its power, upward
Across tilted sand. Unravelled now
And the shore, under its lucid pane,
Clear to the sight, it is spent:
The sun rocks there, as the netted ripple
Into whose skeins the motion threads it
Glances athwart a bed, honey-combed
By heaving stones. Neither survives the instant
But is caught back, and leaves, like the after-image
Released from the floor of a now different mind,
A quick gold, dyeing the uncovering beach
With sunglaze. That which we were,
Confronted by all that we are not,
Grasps in subservience its replenishment.

How Still the Hawk

How still the hawk
Hangs innocent above
Its native wood:
Distance, that purifies the act
Of all intent, has graced
Intent with beauty.
Beauty must lie
As innocence must harm
Whose end (sited,
Held) is naked
Like the map it cowers on.
And the doom drops:
Plummet of peace
To him who does not share
The nearness and the need,
The shrivelled circle
Of magnetic fear.

Winter Encounters

House and hollow; village and valley-side:
    The ceaseless pairings; the interchange
In which the properties are constant
    Resumes its winter starkness. The hedges' barbs
Are bared. Lengthened shadows
    Intersecting, the fields seem parcelled smaller
As if by hedgerow within hedgerow. Meshed
    Into neighbourhood by such shifting ties,
The house reposes, squarely upon its acre

Yet with softened angles, the responsive stone
Changeful beneath the changing light:
    There is a riding-forth, a voyage impending
In this ruffled air, where all moves
    Towards encounter. Inanimate or human,
The distinction fails in these brisk exchanges—
    Say, merely, that the roof greets the cloud,
Or by the wall, sheltering its knot of talkers,
    Encounter enacts itself in the conversation
On customary subjects, where the mind
    May lean at ease, weighing the prospect
Of another's presence. Rain
    And the probability of rain, tares
And their progress through a field of wheat—
    These, though of moment in themselves,
Serve rather to articulate the sense
    That having met, one meets with more
Than the words can witness. One feels behind
    Into the intensity that bodies through them
Calmness within the wind, the warmth in cold.

Northern Spring

Nor is this the setting for extravagance. Trees
Fight with the wind, the wind eludes them
Streaking its cross-lanes over the uneasy water
Whose bronze whitens. To emulate such confusion
One must impoverish the resources of folly,
But to taste it is medicinal. Consider

How through that broken calm, as the sun emerges.
The sky flushes its blue, dyeing the grass
In the promise of a more stable tone:
Less swift however than the cloud is wide—
Its shadow (already) quenching the verdure
As its bulk muffles the sun—the blue drains
And the assault renews in colourless ripples.

Then, lit, the scene deepens. Where should one look
In the profusion of possibilities? One conceives
Placing before them a square house
Washed in the coolness of lime, a hub
For the scattered deployment, to define
In pure white from its verdant ground
The variegated excess which threatens it.

Spring lours. Neither will the summer achieve
That Roman season of an equable province
Where the sun is its own witness and the shadow
Measures its ardour with the impartiality
Of the just. Evening, debauching this sky, asks
To be appraised and to be withstood.

On the Hall at Stowey

Walking by map, I chose unwonted ground,
A crooked, questionable path which led
Beyond the margin, then delivered me
At a turn. Red marl
Had rutted the aimless track   5
That firmly withheld the recompense it hid
Till now, close by its end, the day's discoveries
Began with the dimming night.

A house. The wall-stones, brown.
The doubtful light, more of a mist than light   10
Floating at hedge-height through the sodden fields
Had yielded, or a final glare
Burst there, rather, to concentrate
Sharp saffron, as the ebbing year—
Or so it seemed, for the dye deepened—poured   15
All of its yellow strength through the way I went:

Over grass, garden-space, over the grange
That jutted beyond, lengthening-down
The house line, tall as it was,
By tying it to the earth, trying its pride   20
(Which submitted) under a nest of barns,
A walled weight of lesser encumbrances—
Few of which worsened it, and none
As the iron sheds, sealing my own approach.

All stone. I had passed these last, unwarrantable   25
Symbols of—no;—let me define, rather
The thing they were not, all that we cannot be,
By the description, simply of that which merits it:

Stone. Why must (as it does at each turn)
30 Each day, the mean rob us of patience, distract us
Before even its opposite—before stone, which
Cut, piled, mortared, is patience's presence.

The land farmed, the house was neglected: but
Gashed panes (and there were many) still showed
35 Into the pride of that presence. I had reached
Unchallenged, within feet of the door
Ill-painted, but at no distant date—the least
Our prodigal time could grudge it; paused
To measure the love, to assess its object,
40 That trusts for continuance to the mason's hand.

Five centuries—here were (at the least) five—
In linked love, eager excrescence
Where the door, arched, crowned with acanthus,
Aimed at a civil elegance, but hit
45 This sturdier compromise, neither Greek, Gothic
Nor Strawberry, clumped from the arching-point
And swatheing down, like a fist of wheat,
The unconscious emblem for the house's worth.

Conclusion surrounded it, and the accumulation
50 After Lammas-growth. Still coming on
Heart's-tongue by maiden-hair
Thickened beneath the hedges, the corn levelled
And carried, long-since; but the earth
(Its tint glowed in the house wall)
55 Out of the reddish dark still thrust up foison
Through the browning back of the exhausted year:

Thrust through the unweeded yard, where earth and
    house
Debated the terrain. My eye
Caught in those flags a gravestone's fragment
Set by a careful century. The washed inscription   60
Still keen, showed only by a fragile stem
A stave, a broken circlet, as
(Unintelligibly clear, craft in the sharp decrepitude)
A pothook grooved its firm memorial.

Within, wet from the failing roof,   65
Walls greened. Each hearth re-fitted
For a suburban whim, each room
Denied what it was, diminished thus
To a barbarous mean, had comforted (but for a time)
Its latest tenant. Angered, I turned to my path   70
Through the inhuman light, light that a fish might swim
Stained by the greyness of the smoking fields.

Five centuries. And we? What we had not
Made ugly, we had laid waste—
Left (I should say) the office to nature   75
Whose blind battery, best fitted to perform it
Outdoes us, completes by persistence
All that our negligence fails in. Saddened,
Yet angered beyond sadness, where the road
Doubled upon itself I halted, for a moment
Facing the empty house and its laden barns.

Winter-Piece

You wake, all windows blind—embattled sprays
grained on the medieval glass.
Gates snap like gunshot
as you handle them. Five-barred fragility
sets flying fifteen rooks who go together
silently ravenous above this winter-piece
that will not feed them. They alight
beyond scavenging, missing everything
but the bladed atmosphere, the white resistance.
Ruts with iron flanges track
through a hard decay
where you discern once more
oak-leaf by hawthorn, for the frost
rewhets their edges. In a perfect web
blanched along each spoke
and circle of its woven wheel,
the spider hangs, grasp unbroken
and death-masked in cold. Returning
you see the house glint-out behind
its holed and ragged glaze,
frost-fronds all streaming.

What it was like

It was like the approach of flame
treading the tinder, a fleet
cascade of it taking tree-toll,
halting below the hill and then
covering the corn-field's dryness
in an effortless crescendo. One heard
in the pause of the receding silence
the whole house grow
tense through its ties, the beams
brace beneath pan-tiles
for the coming burst. It came
and went. The blinded pane
emerged from the rainsheet
to an after-water world,
its green confusion brought
closer greener. The baptism
of the shining house was done
and it was like the calm
a church aisle harbours
tasting of incense, space and stone.

How it happened

It happened like this: I heard
from the farm beyond, a grounded
churn go down. The sound
chimed for the wedding of the mind
with what one could not see,
the further fields, the seamless
spread of space, and then,
all bestial ease, the cows
foregathered by the milking place
in a placid stupor. There are two
ways to marry with a land—
first, this bland and blind
submergence of the self, an act
of kind and questionless. The other
is the thing I mean, a whole
event, a happening, the sound
that brings all space in
for its bound, when self is clear
as what we keenest see and hear:
no absolute of eye can tell
the utmost, but the glance
goes shafted from us like a well.

The Snow Fences

They are fencing the upland against
the drifts this wind, those clouds
would bury it under: brow and bone
know already that levelling zero
as you go, an aching skeleton,
in the breathtaking rareness of winter air.

Walking here, what do you see?
Little more, through wind-teased eyes,
than a black, iron tree
and, there, another, a straggle
of low and broken wall between, grass
sapped of its greenness, day going.

The farms are few: spread
as wide, perhaps, as when
the Saxons who found them, chose
these airy and woodless spaces
and froze here before they fed
the unsuperseded burial ground.

Ahead, the church's dead-white
limewash will dazzle the mind
as, dazed, you enter to escape:
despite the stillness here, the chill
of wash-light scarcely seems
less penetrant than the hill-top wind.

Between the graves, you find
a beheaded pigeon, the blood and grain
trailed from its bitten crop, as alien to all

the day's pallor as the raw
wounds of the earth, turned above
a fresh solitary burial.

A plaque of staining metal
distinguishes this grave among
an anonymity whose stones
the frosts have scaled, thrusting under
as if they grudged the ground
its ill-kept memorials.

The bitter darkness drives you
back valleywards, and again you bend
joint and tendon to encounter
the wind's force and leave behind
the nameless stones, the snow-shrouds
of a waste season: they are fencing
the upland against those years, those clouds.

Wind

Insistence being of its nature,
thus a refusal to insist is to meet it
on equal terms. For one is neither
bull to bellow with it, nor barometer
to slide, accommodated, into the mood's trough
once the thing has departed. The woods
shook, as though it were the day
of wrath that furrowed its sentence
in the rippled forms, the bleached
obliquity of the winter grass.

Black branches were staggering
and climbing the air, rattling
on one another like a hailfall:
they clawed and tapped, as if the whole
blind company of the dead
bound in its lime, had risen
to repossess this ground. As if—
but time was in mid-career
streaming through space: the dead
were lying in customary quiet.
Kin to the sole bird abroad
gone tinily over like a flung stone,
one hung there against the wind,
blown to a judgment, yes, brought
to bear fronting the airs' commotion.
The noise above, and the rooted silence
under it, poised one in place,
and time said: 'I rescind
the centuries with now,' and space
banishing one from there to here:
'You are not God. You are not the wind.'

The Weathercocks

Bitten and burned into mirrors of thin gold,
the weathercocks, blind from the weather,
have their days of seeing as they
grind round on their swivels.

A consciousness of pure metal
begins to melt when (say)
that light 'which never was'
begins to be

And catches the snow's accents
in each dip and lap, and the wide
stains on the thawed ploughland are like continents
across a rumpled map.

Their gold eyes hurt
at the corduroy lines come clear whose grain
feels its way over the shapes of the rises
joining one brown accord of stain and stain.

And the patterning stretches, flown
out on a wing of afternoon cloud that the sun
is changing to sea-wet sandflats,
hummocked in tiny dunes like the snow half-gone-

As if the sole wish of the light
were to harrow mind with matter, to shock
wide the glance of the tree-knots and the stone-eyes
the sun is bathing, to waken the weathercocks.

On a Mexican Straw Christ

This is not the event. This
Is a man of straw,
The legs straw-thin
The straw-arms shent
And nailed. And yet this dry
Essence of agony must be
Close-grained to the one
They lifted down, when
Consummatum est the event was done.
Below the baroque straw-
Haloed basket-head
And the crown, far more
Like a cap woven
For a matador than a crown of thorns,
A gap recedes: it makes
A mouth in pain, the teeth
Within its sideways-slashed
And gritted grin, are
Verticals of straw, and they
Emerge where the mask's
Chin ceases and become
Parallels plunging down, their sum
The body of God. Beneath,
Two feet join in one
Cramped culmination, as if
To say: 'I am the un-
Resurrection and the Death.'

On the Tlacolula Bus

On the Tlacolula bus
'I flew for the Fuehrer'
it says: *Yo volé*
para el Fuehrer signed
Lukenbac in Gothic.
The Fuehrer is dead and Lukenbac
does not drive today:
instead, a Mexican with the brown
face of a Mayan
is in his place and under
a sign *No distraer*
al Operador is
chatting across his shoulder.
Would Lukenbac? And does he
care for this country, or long
for a land of hygiene and Christmas trees
where he would not dare
write up his boast in Gothic?
As we swing
out of the market square
a goat on a string
being led by someone
stops, stands and while
the bus passes by
into history, turns
on the succession of windows
its narrow stare, looking
like Lukenbac in exile.

At Barstow

Nervy with neons, the main drag
was all there was. A placeless place.
A faint flavour of Mexico in the tacos
tasting of gasoline. Trucks refuelled
before taking off through space. Someone lived
in the houses with their houseyards wired
like tiny Belsens. The Götterdämmerung
would be like this. No funeral pyres, no choirs
of lost trombones. An Untergang
without a clang, without
a glimmer of gone glory
however dimmed. At the motel desk
was a photograph of Roy Rogers
signed. It was here
he made a stay. He did not
ride away on Trigger
through the high night, the tilted
Pleiades overhead, the polestar low, no
going off until
the eyes of beer-cans
had ceased to glint at him
and the desert darknesses
had quenched the neons. He was spent.
He was content. Down he lay.
The passing trucks patrolled his sleep,
the shifted gears contrived
a muffled fugue against the fading of his day
and his dustless, undishonoured stetson rode
beside the bed,
glowed in the pulsating, never-final twilight
there, at that execrable conjunction
of gasoline and desert air.

Notes

THE ATLANTIC

Study the verse and punctuation, especially of the first lines.

The poem sketches precisely and sensitively the breaking wave. The sea is traditionally an image of infinity, but here, in the endless change of the surf, it represents particularly sharply the *transience* of our experience, our minds, our characters. The whole poem leads up to the last sentence.

HOW STILL THE HAWK

It may be interesting to compare this poem with Ted Hughes's HAWK ROOSTING. Tomlinson's is a difficult poem, very compressed and intellectually strenuous. The conflict between moral or ethical judgments and aesthetic judgments is implied here (lines 4–6), together with the conundrum which natural ferocity (the hawk hanging, the striking) always presents to one who attempts to judge of right and wrong. The poem is terse and tight: the still hawk, the naked target, the swoop—frighteningly clear; the short verse lines have very distinct identity. The last five lines are puzzling (and appear important): who is 'him'? Perhaps it is the passionless observer, at a distance (see lines 4–6), who tends to see the 'aesthetic' beauty of the creature and miss 'the shrivelled circle of magnetic fear'. If this is a right reading, then Tomlinson shows himself here well aware of the need to balance aesthetic and humane pressures.

WINTER ENCOUNTERS

A statement of coherence within life, the interdependence not only of landscape, houses and elements, but also of the people in this setting. One wonders if Tomlinson could say the same of a city community.

The variety and control of the verse are of a high standard.

NORTHERN SPRING

A severely formal statement, which is straightforward if taken slowly. The northern spring, like the northern summer, is unstable and violent: the instability is created for us with a painter's eye (especially in the third verse) and an old-fashioned precision of diction.

ON THE HALL AT STOWEY

1. *unwonted*: not often trodden. Few people now visit the Hall.

4. *marl*: rich soil.

Verse two refers to the yellow light of autumn evening.

18–22. The poet as painter or student of architecture, sensing acutely the pull of 'lines' in the building.

30. *mean*: shallow, vulgar, paltry things, such as our civilization abounds in.

43. *acanthus*: a plant much imitated in ornamental architecture.

46. *Strawberry*: eighteenth-century Gothic architecture, as at Horace Walpole's house at Strawberry Hill.

49. *Conclusion*: autumn.

50. *After Lammas-growth*: growth after ordinary harvest-time.

55. *foison*: abundant growth.

62. *stave*: part of a poetic epitaph.

64. *pothook*: curved flourish in lettering.

The poem is worth comparing with Philip Larkin's CHURCH-GOING: Tomlinson writes as one deeply reverent towards the past and knowledgeable about it; Larkin as one of the suburban characters towards whom Tomlinson feels such anger. Tomlinson, in his donnish parentheses and meticulous phrasing, represents complete defiance of modern streamlined chromium-plated civilization: Larkin an acceptance of it because it is real and is the condition of most people now alive.

WINTER-PIECE

In this and the following poems Tomlinson emerges from his heavy and somewhat academic earlier tone into a crisper, lighter and more concrete way of writing. The painting is more vivid than ever, but the interpretation is now almost entirely suppressed.

HOW IT HAPPENED

Compare the thought behind WINTER ENCOUNTERS; and also, if you are familiar with it, the inscape-poetry of Gerard Manley Hopkins. The poem is as near as Tomlinson comes to a religious statement.

WIND

Compare Ted Hughes's WIND, which Tomlinson is perhaps remembering.

The first six lines are puzzlingly abstract; but read on and the rest of the poem more or less interprets them.

THE WEATHERCOCKS

Verses three, four and five are a weathercock's eye-view.

The whole poem is a magnificent celebration of the patterned richness of the seen world on days of clarity and wind. Celebration with awe: light and colour and line are almost too fierce for the eye, will almost 'melt' and 'waken' even weathercocks.

ON A MEXICAN STRAW CHRIST

Another painting-poem: a poet's version of a great theme of painters.

ON THE TLACOLULA BUS

Almost a political comment, and as such very unusual in Tomlinson's work. It is not, however, the *evil* of Lukenbac's Nazi loyalty that the poet is concerned with, but its futility and grotesque, goat-like pathos.

No distraer al Operador: don't talk to the driver.

Belsen was one of the worst of the concentration camps where millions of Jews were exterminated by the Nazis. The reference to Nazism perhaps suggests the *Götterdämmerung* (twilight of the gods, i.e. the end of all things) and, in turn, *Untergang*—the ultimate 'going-under'.

This is a landscape picture with a difference (it is, of course, a very different kind of landscape from that of the Hall at Stowey)—and we see here a bitter sense of humour which is a new element in Tomlinson's poetry and appears several times in *American Scenes*.

Tony Connor

Tony Connor was born in Lancashire in 1930. He left school at fourteen, since when he has done a variety of jobs. His first book of poetry was published in 1962.

In some respects Connor seems to do for the drab working-class life of England what Philip Larkin does for the drab middle class. Indeed, he shows considerable kinship with a number of poets of the 1950's in England: neat stanzaic verses, ironic restraint, unheroic honesty and an underlying compassion for people. Where he differs from most of the 1950's poets is in his background and subject-matter, and in his air of being a local poet quite prepared to compete with the metropolitans but not to be in awe of them.

As the introductory poem A RATHER PUBLIC STATEMENT suggests, Connor is a moderate and modest poet: this is not a time and I am not the man, he seems to say, for grand pretensions. He is an extremely skilful poet technically, especially in the aptness of his imagery and phrasing; but he has no wish to be flashy. He can write humorously of the Salford landscape, but without sentimentality or frivolity: he knows its ugliness and inadequacy, but it is his home and he writes as one who belongs. His subject is the sort of world in which most people live—the industrial city with massed identical housing, little sense of the past or of landscape—and he faces it fairly, without missionary zeal or aesthetic apathy. At its worst, he shows us, it is still life, a world of people and things no less real than any other.

A Rather Public Statement

I do not intend to contribute
a single line, any half-heard
snatch of mystery
to the street's chronicle.
I am deaf among men;
I am dumb among women;
I am the prince of never-there,
the master of winter.

I have no knowledge to offer
about the marriage bed,
nor am I able to say
where, or why important
decisions were made
affecting the lives
of all who heard them
and many more who did not.

I will not pretend an ability
to judge character from faces;
darkness frightens me
and I am apprehensive in sunlight.
Nevertheless,
mine was the bland smile,
the fur coat of incomprehension
in the catastrophe.

When the trek ended, frustrated
by the abattoir wall,
and the disgusted others
started rewinding the string,

I was in the chip shop
ordering fourpenn'orth.
I had not come all that way
for nothing.

On certain nights I have discerned
complicated patterns
in smudged penumbras,
but have never missed my supper.
The voices from alleys
—loving or hating—
I have accepted as part
of a wholesome definition.

You will appreciate my reluctance
to give you directions:
my inability to reach
the homes of others
is widely known—
although one of my hobbies
is studying maps
in the front room.

Finally, let me assure those
who imagine me lending a willing ear,
that my lopsided appearance
is congenital,
and should not be interpreted
as a leaning
towards anything
other than the ground.

October in Clowes Park

The day dispossessed of light. At four o'clock
in the afternoon, a sulphurous, manufactured
twilight, smudging the scummed lake's far side,
leant on the park. Sounds, muffled—
as if the lolling muck clogged them at the source—
crawled to the ear. A skyed ball thudded
to ground, a swan leathered its wings by the island.
I stood and watched a water-hen arrow
shutting silver across the sooty mat
of the lake's surface, an earl's lake,
though these fifty years the corporation's,
and what is left of the extensive estate—
a few acres of scruffy, flat land
framing this wet sore in the minds of property agents—
a public park. All else is built on.
Through swags of trees poked the bare backsides
of encircling villas, garages, gardening-sheds,
a ring of lights making the park dimmer.
Boys and men shouldering long rods—
all licensed fishers, by their open way—
scuffled the cinders past me, heading for home,
but I stayed on; the dispossessed day
held me, turned me towards the ruined Hall.
Pulsing in that yellow, luminous, murk
(a trick of the eye), the bits of broken pillar
built into banks, the last upright wall,
the stalactite-hung split shells of stables,
seemed likely to find a voice—such pent-in grief
and anger!—or perhaps to explode silently
with force greater than any known to progress,
wiping the district, town, kingdom, age,

to darkness far deeper than that which fluffed
now at the neat new urinal's outline,
and heaved and beat behind it in the ruins.
Like a thud in the head, suddenly become memory,
stillness was dumb around me. Scrambling up
a heap of refuse, I grabbed at crystalled brick.
Flakes fell from my hand—a gruff tinkle—
no knowledge there of what brought the Hall low,
or concern either. Neither did I care.
Irrecoverably dead, slumped in rank weed
and billowy grass, it mouldered from here to now,
connoting nothing but where my anger stood
and grief enough to pull the sagging smoke down
from the sky, a silent, lethal, swaddling
over the garden I played in as a child,
and over those children—laughter in the branches—
shaking the pear-tree's last sour fruit to ground.

St. Mark's, Cheetham Hill

Designed to dominate the district—
God being nothing if not large
and stern, melancholic from man's fall
(like Victoria widowed early)—
the church, its yard, were raised on a plateau
six feet above the surrounding green.
There weren't many houses then; Manchester
was a good walk away. I've seen
faded photographs: the church standing
amidst strolling gentry, as though
ready to sail for the Empire's farthest parts;—
the union jack at the tower's masthead
enough to quell upstart foreigners and natives.
But those were the early days. The city
began to gollop profits, burst
outward on all sides. Soon,
miles of the cheapest brick swaddled landmarks,
the church one. Chimes that had used to wake
workers in Whitefield, died in near streets.

From our house—a part of the parish—
St. Mark's is a turn right, a turn left,
and straight down Coke Street past the Horseshoe.
The raised graveyard—full these many years—
overlooks the junction of five streets;
pollarded plane trees round its edge,
the railings gone to help fight Hitler.
Adam Murray of New Galloway,
'Who much improved the spinning mule',
needs but a step from his tomb to peer in
at somebody's glittering television;

Harriet Pratt, 'A native of Derby',
might sate her judgment-hunger with chips
were she to rise and walk twenty yards.
The houses are that close. The church,
begrimed, an ugly irregular box
squatting above those who once filled it
with faith and praise, looks smaller now
than in those old pictures. Subdued
by a raincoat factory's bulk, the Kosher
Slaughter House next door, its dignity
is rare weddings, the Co-op hearse,
and hired cars full of elderly mourners.
The congregations are tiny these days;
few folk could tell you whether it's 'High' or 'Low';
the vicar's name, the times of services,
is specialized knowledge. And fear has gone;
the damp, psalmed, God of my childhood has gone.
Perhaps a boy delivering papers
in winter darkness before the birds wake,
keeps to Chapel Street's far side, for fear
some corpse interred at his ankle's depth
might shove a hand through the crumbling wall
and grab him in passing; but not for fear
of black religion—the blurred bulk
of God in drizzle and dirty mist,
or hooded with snow on his white throne
watching the sparrow fall.
                              Now, the graveyard,
its elegant wrought-ironwork wrenched,
carted away; its rhymed epitaphs,
urns of stone and ingenious scrolls,
chipped, tumbled, masked by weeds,
is used as a playground. Shouting children
Tiggy between the tombs.

On Saturdays

I walk there sometimes—through the drift
of jazz from open doors, the tide
of frying fish, and the groups of women
gossiping on their brushes—to see the church,
its God decamped, or dead, or daft
to all but the shrill hosannas of children
whose prayers are laughter, playing such parts
in rowdy games, you'd think it built
for no greater purpose, think its past
one long term of imprisonment.

There's little survives Authority's cant
that's not forgotten, written-off,
or misunderstood. The Methodist Chapel's
been bought by the Jews for a Synagogue;
Ukrainian Catholics have the Wesleyan's
sturdy structure built to outlast Rome—
which clings to its holy snowball down the street;
and men of the district say St. Mark's
is part of a clearance area. Soon
it will be down as low as rubble
from every house that squeezed it round,
to bed a motorway and a new estate.
Or worse: repainted, pointed, primmed—
as becomes a unit in town-planners'
clever dreams of a healthy community—
will prosper in dignity and difference,
the gardened centre of new horizons.

Rather than this, I'd see it smashed,
and picture the final splendours of decay:
Opposing gangs in wild 'Relievo',
rushing down aisles and dusty pews

83

at which the houses look straight in
past broken wall; and late-night drunkards
stumbling their usual short-cut home
across uneven eulogies, fumbling
difficult flies to pour discomfort out
in comfortable shadows, in a nave
they praise with founts, and moonlit blooms of steam.

Elegy for Alfred Hubbard

Hubbard is dead, the old plumber;
who will mend our burst pipes now,
the tap that has dripped all the summer,
testing the sink's overflow?

No other like him. Young men with knowledge
of new techniques, theories from books,
may better his work straight from college,
but who will challenge his squint-eyed looks

in kitchen, bathroom, under floorboards,
rules of thumb which were often wrong;
seek as erringly stopcocks in cupboards,
or make a job last half as long?

He was a man who knew the ginnels,
alleyways, streets—the whole district,
family secrets, minor annals,
time-honoured fictions fused to fact.

Seventy years of gossip muttered
under his cap, his tufty thatch,
so that his talk was slow and clotted,
hard to follow, and too much.

As though nothing fell, none vanished,
and time were the maze of Cheetham Hill,
in which the dead—with jobs unfinished—
waited to hear him ring the bell.

For much he never got round to doing,
but meant to, when weather bucked up,
or worsened, or when his pipe was drawing,
or when he'd finished this cup.

I thought time, he forgot so often,
had forgotten him, but here's Death's pomp
over his house, and by the coffin
the son who will inherit his blowlamp,

tools, workshop, cart, and cornet
(pride of Cheetham Prize Brass Band),
and there's his mourning widow, Janet,
stood at the gate he'd promised to mend.

Soon he will make his final journey;
shaved and silent, strangely trim,
with never a pause to talk to any-
body: how arrow-like, for him!

In St. Mark's Church, whose dismal tower
he pointed and painted when a lad,
they will sing his praises amidst flowers
while, somewhere, a cellar starts to flood,

and the housewife banging his front-door knocker
is not surprised to find him gone,
and runs for Thwaite, who's a better worker,
and sticks at a job until it's done.

Child's Bouncing Song

Molly Vickers
wets her knickers,
Georgie's father's big and black,
cream on Sunday
milk on Monday,
I'm the cock of all the back.

Tell me who's a
bigger boozer
Mister Baker beats them all,
from his lorry
watch him hurry,
touch the ground and touch the wall.

Who're the gentry
down our entry—
Mrs. Smith's got two T.V.'s.
What if her coat
is a fur coat,
all her kids are full of fleas.

Joan loves Harry,
Jack will marry
Edna when they both grow up,
I'll announce it,
bounce bounce bounce it,
our dog Whiskers had a pup.

High and low and
to and fro and
down the street and up the hill,

Mrs. Cuthbert's
husband snuffed it,
she got nothing from his will.

Mister, mister,
Shirley's sister
won a prize on Blackpool prom,
mam'll smother
our kid brother
when the school inspectors come.

Skip and hopping
I'm off shopping,
Tuesday night it's pie for tea,
please to take this
ball and make this
song of bouncing song for me.

Lancashire Winter

The town remembers no such plenty,
under the wind from off the moor.
The labour exchange is nearly empty;
stiletto heels on the Palais floor
move between points of patent leather.
Sheepskin coats keep out the weather.

Commerce and Further Education
won't be frozen. Dully free
in snack bars and classrooms sits the patient
centrally heated peasantry,
receiving Wimpies like the Host;
striving to get That Better Post.

Snow on the streets and Mini-Minors
thickens to drifts, and in the square,
from grubby plinths, blind eyes, stone collars,
the fathers of revolution stare,
who, against pikes and burning brands,
built the future with bare hands.

A Woman Dying

In a room with a wardrobe far too large—
bought at a sale cheap, or handed down—
this careless woman struggled for breath.
Faded oilcloth stopped short of the skirting boards;
beneath her pyjama-top there flowered
the vivid, cancerous sores. She lay with death.

Chrysanthemums in a white bowl
held their tongues, were not telling the name
of whoever had brought them. Now and then
neighbours and friends appeared to be by her side.
Her husband came, spoke, went,—so did the pain;
nightdark, daylight, nightdark, and daylight again.

Already nothingness hung like a smell
among the factual furniture. The bare
bulb in its rusty socket rocked
substance away as her younger sister slept.
'Is that burglars?' she said in the small hours,
who had never worried whether the door was locked.

Something was different; something had come in
through fifty-six years of doors left on the latch,
that fed on neglected duties: dust
gathering unswept, meals she'd forgotten to make.
Perhaps it would go if she did her best:
on tiny observances she fretted dully and fussed.

But could not make redress, nor pay
attention enough to keep her sister's face
sharp as her memory of it. Trees

beyond the window waved branches of good-bye,
and then: 'What was it the branches waved?'
Question and answer were like as two peas.

And neither mattered. The pain blanked out
everything but a lusting after death,
or youth, or sleep—they looked the same.
Whatever knew friendly flesh was good, was God.
She choked and spat and coughed and tore
down Heaven with moans until the doctor came.

A needle eased the world away.
She did not see the window's curdled shine
grow fronds and flowers which multiplied
all night despite that thrusting, fiery, breath.
At dawn winter went on without her,
while by the bed her sister stood and cried.

Mrs. Root

Busybody, nosey-parker
lacking the vast discretion of most
was this woman. The self-cast
chief mourner at funerals, worker
at weddings, she could sniff out death
in a doctor's optimism, joggle
a maiden's mind (button-holed on the front path)
till virginity bit like filed teeth.

Prepared, without discrimination,
friend and enemy for the grave.
Washed, talcumed them all. A woman
who wore such ceremonies like a glove,
could console a grief-struck household
that hardly knew her name, and then
collect money for a wreath fit to wield
at a Queen's passing. Death-skilled
but no less wedding-wise,
her hand stitched the perfecting dart
in bridal satin; she brought report
of cars arriving, clear skies
towards the church. They were her tears
(pew-stifled) from which the happiest
laughter billowed confetti outside the black doors.
Of best wishes, loudest were hers.

And nobody thanked her; Why doesn't
she mind her own business? they said
who'd leant upon her. Crude and peasant-like
her interest in brides, and the dead.
I thought so too, yet still was loath

to add my voice, sensing that
my secret poems were like her actions: both
pried into love and savoured death.

An Evening at Home

Sensing a poem about to happen,
two letters demanded to be written.

One to a man about a dog
began clearly and ended vaguely;

the other, to a girl for old times' sake,
overstepped the bounds of propriety. My teeth began to
    ache.

From a single suspect raw-edged tooth
the pain spread all over my mouth

before I could stop it. Coupled with
rising flatulence, it nearly overcame faith

in my sacred calling. But I fought
with a concentration of poetic thought

upon my desk. I almost went over
from the chair in which I'd sat to recover—

and would have done had not the lodger knocked
to say that his sink waste-pipe was blocked.

Using the plunger, I began to feel jaded
and disillusioned; something more was needed

than mere poems to right the world.
My hands were numb; I remembered the millions killed

in God's name; I remembered bombs, gas-chambers,
        famine, poverty,
and my greying hair. I could not write poetry.

My nose tingled as though it was going to bleed;
I shut my notebook quietly and went to bed.

Notes

A RATHER PUBLIC STATEMENT

A rejection of the claims artists tend to make. Not only does Connor see himself as, in Wordsworthian terms, a man amongst men, but also as an undistinguished man. He identifies himself even with 'the bland smile,/the fur coat of incomprehension/in the catastrophe': which is presumably a reference to the supposed apathy of people today in the face of political manœuvring or hydrogen-bomb warfare. The fourth verse is obscure, but I suspect some allusion to the inhumanities committed by man to man (for example, under Nazism)—the poet does not absolve himself from guilt. He may have sensed at times (fifth verse) magnificent Patterns— the key to life, a hope for humanity, and all that—but only in blurred shadow, and even then he has not got particularly excited over it. The love and the hate, the evil and the good, are a part of life. He would like to think he could penetrate and understand the lives of others, but has no illusions about his limitations in that direction; and he refuses to be considered a saintly, compassionate receiver of men's problems.

The tone is that of whimsy, but it is a serious poem and a refreshingly honest one.

OCTOBER IN CLOWES PARK

This is masterly descriptive writing, as readers in the Midlands and the North will recognize at once: such parks are features of our large industrial cities. It is a painting, and a comment of painstaking detail at the same time. As with many of Connor's poems, the emotional debate is delicately balanced: the squalor *is* foul, the decay depressing, the poet's anger real; but the ruins and the squalor have their own unhealthy glamour (they have what O Level English papers call 'Atmosphere')—not least in the nostalgia for childhood which they awaken in the poet.

ST. MARK'S, CHEETHAM HILL
A sociological and historical study, redeemed by a sad humour and affection which sociologists and historians might disapprove. Here the poet, who in OCTOBER IN CLOWES PARK seemed appalled by the present day, has no regrets for the bad old past and is depressed by the thoughts of a hygienic synthetic future: he writes of the present-day muddle and anachronisms with warm relish. The last paragraph is an impudent gesture in the same spirit.

ELEGY FOR ALFRED HUBBARD
An understandably popular anthology piece: Connor as the John Betjeman of Cheetham Hill. Again, the balance between humour and seriousness, sentimentality and irony, is nicely poised.

LANCASHIRE WINTER
A poem of the 1960's and comparative prosperity, in an area of Britain which has known years of deprivation and social struggle. Was this, though, the future the fathers of revolution fought to build?

A WOMAN DYING
A completely straight and sober poem on a subject which most writers (and people) instinctively avoid. The poet who claimed (in A RATHER PUBLIC STATEMENT) that 'my inability to reach/the homes of others/is widely known' here achieves an extraordinary and moving discovery of a very different consciousness from his own. It is hard, painful writing, but writing of great delicacy.

MRS. ROOT
Working-class life tends to be more corporate than middle-class life, and—in the past at least—most blocks of streets had

their Mrs. Roots. The poem is a sympathetic (but, as usual, balanced) study of such a woman, with a personal note at the end which charges the poem with an unexpected significance. Consider A WOMAN DYING in the light of the last few lines of this poem.

AN EVENING AT HOME
We have seen that Connor is fundamentally a serious, even dedicated poet—but also that he has a horror of over-solemnity, and a more penetrating honesty than most. This poem is more or less light-hearted, but the lines about 'the millions killed in God's name' cannot be too easily shrugged off. If the poem is, like many of Connor's, about his own inadequacy, he can still not be accused of glorying in it.

Ted Hughes

Ted Hughes was born in 1930 in Mytholmroyd in Yorkshire. He began to make a reputation as a poet while an undergraduate at Cambridge; and his first book of poems, *The Hawk in the Rain* (1957) earned him rapid recognition. Since then he has published several other volumes of poetry and a number of books for children, and has done a good deal of broadcasting, especially for schools. He was married to the American poet Sylvia Plath, who died in 1963. Ted Hughes is the best known of the younger English poets: his work can be quickly apprehended and speaks with unmistakable vigour and vividness, which the average reader welcomes after the extreme difficulty of many of his more important predecessors this century.

One reason why Hughes is not difficult is that, superficially at least, he is not an innovator but a traditionalist. Or, to put it another way, he is an English poet with roots in English diction, English literature, English things: the impact of Americans and Continentals upon our literature in the last 150 years has largely missed Hughes, whose response to experience is refreshingly direct. Landscape, animals, working life, living language: it is in these that Hughes discovers his distinctive voice, not in his literary studies. What one notices first in Hughes is comparatively violent sensuous experience, as it has rarely been expressed in poetry since Shakespeare and Ben Jonson: this he shares with D. H. Lawrence, whose animal poems are the only close antecedents for those of Hughes (the jaguar, the hawk, the pike and others) which have earned him his greatest popularity.

The other poet to whom Hughes seems to owe something is the nineteenth-century poet Gerard Manley Hopkins. Both seek out the rougher, Scandinavian elements of our language, which are significantly more prominent in northern England than in the south: the monosyllabic words of concrete experience, heavy with consonantal clatter. At times, in his excitement at a refreshed, reinvigorated language, Hughes overdoes it: he shouts and gesticulates to the point of inflation. It sometimes seems that one Hughes poem is rather like another, and that it is the first discovery of his work that is most exciting.

But it is the less superficial aspects of Hughes's poetry which are, in the long run, most interesting: and here he shows, after all, some kinship with his contemporaries, in other countries as well as in England. First, whatever his diction or subject-matter, Hughes writes poems which are entirely of our time in their brusqueness, and their quality of enigma. Where artists of the past instinctively took it upon themselves to interpret, to explain, and even to classify, artists of the mid-twentieth century seem more and more reluctant to venture explicit comment or theory. Experience is presented, with more ambiguity and complexity—and consequently more reality—than ever before; and the poem stops. The first poem in this Hughes selection—THE BULL MOSES— illustrates this clearly enough. It is a kind of poetry which Americans—Wallace Stevens and Louis Simpson are two who appear in this series—have developed more than Englishmen; and Hughes seems to sense that modern American verse has more to offer him than modern English. Some recent Hughes poems such as FULL MOON AND LITTLE FRIEDA or A WIND FLASHES THE GRASS suggest that the poet is exploring further this apparently fragmentary manner.

Associated in part with this stopping-short of interpretation, this respectful bewilderment in the face of the complexity of things, is a preoccupation with the weird, the occult, the supernatural. There is much in common here between the poetry of Hughes and that of his wife Sylvia Plath. Life is never simple or safe, in Hughes's view: never all, or merely all, it seems to be. The last stanzas of PIKE are written in almost the terms of a horror story: the bull Moses has

the weight of the sun and the moon and the world
hammered
To a ring of brass through his nostrils.

The wind in WIND 'flexing like the lens of a mad eye'; the delirious horror of SUNSTROKE; the ploughman's terror at awareness of past and future in A WIND FLASHES THE GRASS: these are a part of Hughes's poetry as vital as the harsh diction and the 'feeling for' animals. Indeed his is rarely a feeling *for* animals, more often a sense of awe before their non-human personalities. It may not be too much to say that in places Hughes is trying to achieve a modern re-statement of the concept of natural evil.

The Thought-Fox

I imagine this midnight moment's forest:
Something else is alive
Beside the clock's loneliness
And this blank page where my fingers move.

Through the window I see no star:
Something more near
Though deeper within darkness
Is entering the loneliness:

Cold, delicately as the dark snow,
A fox's nose touches twig, leaf;
Two eyes serve a movement, that now
And again now, and now, and now

Sets neat prints into the snow
Between trees, and warily a lame
Shadow lags by stump and in hollow
Of a body that is bold to come

Across clearings, an eye,
A widening deepening greenness,
Brilliantly, concentratedly,
Coming about its own business

Till, with a sudden sharp hot stink of fox
It enters the dark hole of the head.
The window is starless still; the clock ticks,
The page is printed.

The Bull Moses

A hoist up and I could lean over
The upper edge of the high half-door,
My left foot ledged on the hinge, and look in at the byre's
Blaze of darkness: a sudden shut-eyed look
Backward into the head.

        Blackness is depth
Beyond star. But the warm weight of his breathing,
The ammoniac reek of his litter, the hotly-tongued
Mash of his cud, steamed against me.
Then, slowly, as onto the mind's eye—
The brow like masonry, the deep-keeled neck:
Something come up there onto the brink of the gulf,
Hadn't heard of the world, too deep in itself to be called to,
Stood in sleep. He would swing his muzzle at a fly
But the square of sky where I hung, shouting, waving,
Was nothing to him; nothing of our light
Found any reflection in him.

        Each dusk the farmer led him
Down to the pond to drink and smell the air,
And he took no pace but the farmer
Led him to take it, as if he knew nothing
Of the ages and continents of his fathers,
Shut, while he wombed, to a dark shed
And steps between his door and the duckpond;
The weight of the sun and the moon and the world
    hammered
To a ring of brass through his nostrils.

He would raise
His streaming muzzle and look out over the meadows,
But the grasses whispered nothing awake, the fetch
Of the distance drew nothing to momentum
In the locked black of his powers. He came strolling
    gently back,
Paused neither towards the pig-pens on his right,
Nor towards the cow-byres on his left: something
Deliberate in his leisure, some beheld future
Founding in his quiet.

           I kept the door wide,
Closed it after him and pushed the bolt.

View of a Pig

The pig lay on a barrow dead.
It weighed, they said, as much as three men.
Its eyes closed, pink white eyelashes.
Its trotters stuck straight out.

Such weight and thick pink bulk
Set in death seemed not just dead.
It was less than lifeless, further off.
It was like a sack of wheat.

I thumped it without feeling remorse.
One feels guilty insulting the dead,
Walking on graves. But this pig
Did not seem able to accuse.

It was too dead. Just so much
A poundage of lard and pork.
Its last dignity had entirely gone.
It was not a figure of fun.

Too dead now to pity.
To remember its life, din, stronghold
Of earthly pleasure as it had been,
Seemed a false effort, and off the point.

Too deadly factual. Its weight
Oppressed me—how could it be moved?
And the trouble of cutting it up!
The gash in its throat was shocking, but not pathetic.

Once I ran at a fair in the noise
To catch a greased piglet
That was faster and nimbler than a cat,
Its squeal was the rending of metal.

Pigs must have hot blood, they feel like ovens.
Their bite is worse than a horse's—
They chop a half-moon clean out.
They eat cinders, dead cats.

Distinctions and admirations such
As this one was long finished with.
I stared at it a long time. They were going to scald it,
Scald it and scour it like a doorstep.

Pike

Pike, three inches long, perfect
Pike in all parts, green tigering the gold.
Killers from the egg: the malevolent aged grin.
They dance on the surface among the flies.

Or move, stunned by their own grandeur,
Over a bed of emerald, silhouette
Of submarine delicacy and horror.
A hundred feet long in their world.

In ponds, under the heat-struck lily pads—
Gloom of their stillness:
Logged on last year's black leaves, watching upwards.
Or hung in an amber cavern of weeds.

The jaws' hooked clamp and fangs
Not to be changed at this date;
A life subdued to its instrument;
The gills kneading quietly, and the pectorals.

Three we kept behind glass,
Jungled in weed; three inches, four,
And four and a half: fed fry to them—
Suddenly there were two. Finally one

With a sag belly and the grin it was born with.
And indeed they spare nobody.
Two, six pounds each, over two feet long,
High and dry and dead in the willow-herb—

One jammed past its gills down the other's gullet:
The outside eye stared: as a vice locks—
The same iron in this eye
Though its film shrank in death.

The pond I fished, fifty yards across,
Whose lilies and muscular tench
Had outlasted every visible stone
Of the monastery that planted them—

Stilled legendary depth:
It was as deep as England. It held
Pike too immense to stir, so immense and old
That past nightfall I dared not cast

But silently cast and fished
With the hair frozen on my head
For what might move, for what eye might move.
The still splashes on the dark pond,

Owls hushing the floating woods
Frail on my ear against the dream
Darkness beneath night's darkness had freed,
That rose slowly towards me, watching.

The Jaguar

The apes yawn and adore their fleas in the sun.
The parrots shriek as if they were on fire, or strut
Like cheap tarts to attract the stroller with the nut.
Fatigued with indolence, tiger and lion

Lie still as the sun. The boa-constrictor's coil
Is a fossil. Cage after cage seems empty, or
Stinks of sleepers from the breathing straw.
It might be painted on a nursery wall.

But who runs like the rest past these arrives
At a cage where the crowd stands, stares, mesmerized,
As a child at a dream, at a jaguar hurrying enraged
Through prison darkness after the drills of his eyes

On a short fierce fuse. Not in boredom—
The eye satisfied to be blind in fire,
By the bang of blood in the brain deaf the ear—
He spins from the bars, but there's no cage to him

More than to the visionary his cell:
His stride is wildernesses of freedom:
The world rolls under the long thrust of his heel.
Over the cage floor the horizons come.

Second Glance at a Jaguar

Skinful of bowls, he bowls them,
The hip going in and out of joint, dropping the spine
With the urgency of his hurry
Like a cat going along under thrown stones, under cover,
Glancing sideways, running
Under his spine. A terrible, stump-legged waddle
Like a thick Aztec disemboweller,
Club-swinging, trying to grind some square
Socket between his hind legs round,
Carrying his head like a brazier of spilling embers,
And the black bit of his mouth, he takes it
Between his back teeth, he has to wear his skin out,
He swipes a lap at the water-trough as he turns,
Swivelling the ball of his heel on the polished spot,
Showing his belly like a butterfly,
At every stride he has to turn a corner
In himself and correct it. His head
Is like the worn down stump of another whole jaguar,
His body is just the engine shoving it forward,
Lifting the air up and shoving on under,
The weight of his fangs hanging the mouth open,
Bottom jaw combing the ground. A gorged look,
Gangster, club-tail lumped along behind gracelessly,
He's wearing himself to heavy ovals,
Muttering some mantrah, some drum-song of murder
To keep his rage brightening, making his skin
Intolerable, spurred by the rosettes, the cain-brands,
Wearing the spots off from the inside,
Rounding some revenge. Going like a prayer-wheel,
The head dragging forward, the body keeping up,

The hind legs lagging. He coils, he flourishes
The blackjack tail, as if looking for a target,
Hurrying through the underworld, soundless.

Hawk Roosting

I sit in the top of the wood, my eyes closed.
Inaction, no falsifying dream
Between my hooked head and hooked feet:
Or in sleep rehearse perfect kills and eat.

The convenience of the high trees!
The air's buoyancy and the sun's ray
Are of advantage to me;
And the earth's face upward for my inspection.

My feet are locked upon the rough bark.
It took the whole of Creation
To produce my foot, my each feather:
Now I hold Creation in my foot

Or fly up, and revolve it all slowly—
I kill where I please because it is all mine.
There is no sophistry in my body:
My manners are tearing off heads—

The allotment of death.
For the one path of my flight is direct
Through the bones of the living.
No arguments assert my right:

The sun is behind me.
Nothing has changed since I began.
My eye has permitted no change.
I am going to keep things like this.

Wind

This house has been far out at sea all night,
The woods crashing through darkness, the booming hills,
Winds stampeding the fields under the window
Floundering black astride and blinding wet

Till day rose; then under an orange sky
The hills had new places, and wind wielded
Blade-like, luminous black and emerald,
Flexing like the lens of a mad eye.

At noon I scaled along the house-side as far as
The coal-house door. I dared once to look up—
Through the brunt wind that dented the balls of my eyes
The tent of the hills drummed and strained its guyrope,

The fields quivering, the skyline a grimace,
At any second to bang and vanish with a flap:
The wind flung a magpie away and a black-
Back gull bent like an iron bar slowly. The house

Rang like some fine green goblet in the note
That any second would shatter it. Now deep
In chairs, in front of the great fire, we grip
Our hearts and cannot entertain book, thought,

Or each other. We watch the fire blazing,
And feel the roots of the house move, but sit on,
Seeing the window tremble to come in,
Hearing the stones cry out under the horizons.

Sunstroke

Frightening the blood in its tunnel
The mowing machine ate at the field of grass.

My eyes had been glared dark. Through a red heat
The cradled guns, damascus, blued, flared—

At every stir sliding their molten embers
Into my head. Sleekly the clover

Bowed and flowed backward
Over the saw-set swimming blades

Till the blades bit—roots, stones, ripped into red—
Some baby's body smoking among the stalks.

Reek of paraffin and creosote
Swabbing my lungs doctored me back

Laid on a sack in the great-beamed engine-shed.
I drank at stone, at iron of plough and harrow;

Dulled in a pit, heard thick walls of rain
And voices in swaddled confinement near me

Warm as veins. I lay healing
Under the ragged length of a dog fox

That dangled head downward from one of the beams,
With eyes open, forepaws strained at a leap—

Also surprised by the rain.

November

The month of the drowned dog. After long rain the land
Was sodden as the bed of an ancient lake,
Treed with iron and birdless. In the sunk lane
The ditch—a seep silent all summer—

Made brown foam with a big voice: that, and my boots
On the lane's scrubbed stones, in the gulleyed leaves,
Against the hill's hanging silence;
Mist silvering the droplets on the bare thorns

Slower than the change of daylight.
In a let of the ditch a tramp was bundled asleep:
Face tucked down into beard, drawn in
Under its hair like a hedgehog's. I took him for dead,

But his stillness separated from the death
Of the rotting grass and the ground. A wind chilled,
And a fresh comfort tightened through him,
Each hand stuffed deeper into the other sleeve.

His ankles, bound with sacking and hairy band,
Rubbed each other, resettling. The wind hardened;
A puff shook a glittering from the thorns,
And again the rain's dragging grey columns

Smudged the farms. In a moment
The fields were jumping and smoking; the thorns
Quivered, riddled with the glassy verticals.
I stayed on under the welding cold

Watching the tramp's face glisten and the drops on his
    coat
Flash and darken. I thought what strong trust
Slept in him—as the trickling furrows slept,
And the thorn-roots in their grip on darkness;

And the buried stones, taking the weight of winter;
The hill where the hare crouched with clenched teeth.
Rain plastered the land till it was shining
Like hammered lead, and I ran, and in the rushing wood

Shuttered by a black oak leaned.
The keeper's gibbet had owls and hawks
By the neck, weasels, a gang of cats, crows:
Some, stiff, weightless, twirled like dry bark bits

In the drilling rain. Some still had their shape,
Had their pride with it; hung, chins on chests,
Patient to outwait these worst days that beat
Their crowns bare and dripped from their feet.

You Drive in a Circle

Slowly a hundred miles through the powerful rain.

Your clothes are towelled with sweat and the car-glass
   sweats,
And there is a smell of damp dog.
Rain-sog is rotting your shoes to paper.

Over old hairy moors, a dark Arctic depths, cresting
   under rain,
Where the road topples, plunging with its crazed rigging
Like a racketty iron tanker

Into a lunge of spray, emerges again—
Through hard rending of water,
Drowned eyes at the melting windshield,

Out above the swamped moor-wallows, the mist-gulfs of
   no-thinking.
Down in there are the sheep, rooted like sponges,
Chewing and digesting and undeterred.

What could they lose, however utterly they drowned?
Already sodden as they are with the world, like fossils,
And what is not the world is God, a starry comforter of
   good blood.

Where are you heading? Everything is already here.
Your hardest look cannot anchor out among these rocks,

Your coming days cannot anchor among these torn
    clouds that cannot anchor.

Your destination waits where you left it.

Full Moon and little Frieda

A cool small evening shrunk to a dog bark and the clank
    of a bucket—

And you listening.
A spider's web, tense for the dew's touch.
A pail lifted, still and brimming—mirror
To tempt a first star to a tremor.

Cows are going home in the lane there, looping the
    hedges with their warm wreaths of breath—
A dark river of blood, many boulders,
Balancing unspilled milk.

'Moon!' you cry suddenly, 'Moon! Moon!'

The moon has stepped back like an artist gazing amazed
    at a work
That points at him amazed.

A Wind Flashes the Grass

Leaves pour blackly across.
We cling to the earth, with glistening eyes, pierced afresh
      by the tree's cry.

And the incomprehensible cry
From the boughs, in the wind
Sets us listening for below words,
Meanings that will not part from the rock.

The trees thunder in unison, on a gloomy afternoon,
And the ploughman grows anxious, his tractor becomes
      terrible,
As his memory litters downwind
And the shadows of his bones toss darkly on the air.

The trees suddenly storm to a stop, in a hush,
Against the sky, where the field ends,
And crowd there, shuddering
And wary, like horses bewildered by lightning.

The stirring of their twigs against the dark, travelling sky
Is the oracle of the earth.

They too are afraid they too are momentary
Streams rivers of shadow.

Notes

THE THOUGHT-FOX

A poem about writing a poem. The poem is first sensed, but
not there: gradually it emerges, suddenly it happens. The
fox, then, is a symbol, or an extended metaphor: but it is
itself created with great precision and immediacy. Which is
more vivid, the poet's study or the forest and fox? The
'imagined world' is perhaps more powerful than the 'actual'.

Hughes is a skilful handler of half-rhyme and assonance as
an alternative to the strictly limited chiming of full rhyme. He
also shows, particularly in his early work, an allegiance to the
four-line stanza even while frequently running-on into the
next stanza. The total effect is one of control without cer-
tainty; of exploration rather than arrival. THE THOUGHT-FOX,
it is true, comes to a satisfactory end; but fundamentally it is
a puzzled poem, trying to come to terms with a mystery.

THE BULL MOSES

byre: cattle-shed.

The bull seems foreign to the mortal world, of light and
normality: a dull god for whom the child, hanging on the
shed door, had no difficulty feeling awe. The awe is re-
created and, I find, transmitted in the poem . . . and then the
poet, almost painfully, dismisses it in the humdrum facts of
the last line and a half.

VIEW OF A PIG

A poem of bewilderment. 'I stared at it a long time.' The
greased piglet at the fair and the thumpable carcass at the
market: that they should be the same thing is incredible. The
poem is mainly concerned with the great dead weight of the
carcass: note the clipped, heavy sentences (the poem has an

extraordinary proportion of full-stops to lines), and phrases which carry in their sound the suggestion of their subject: 'stuck straight out' . . . 'thick pink bulk'.

The bewilderment is not that of violent emotion, but of absence of emotion. A dead pig ought to be either tragic, solemn, being dead; or comic, being a pig. It is neither.

The first sentence of the last verse means: 'I have just listed distinctions (of pigs) and admirations (which I feel) of a sort which this particular pig would have nothing further to do with.' The poet saves his most forceful image for the end, and slaps it down to confirm finally what he has been saying throughout the poem: what could be flatter, heavier, deader than a doorstep?

PIKE

A consideration of evil, in the natural world where distinctions of good and evil normally seem irrelevant.

THE JAGUAR

One of the clearest and most skilful of Hughes's studies of ferocity. Note the double appropriateness of the descriptive images: 'as if they were on fire' and 'like cheap tarts' describe not only the noise and movement of the parrots, but also their colour: the comparison of 'the boa-constrictor's coil' to a fossil shows us not only its stillness but also its texture. The verse too is immensely skilful—the mid-line full-stops serve real purpose, first by bringing the verse, appropriately, almost to a standstill (stanza two), and secondly, by highlighting the sharp hissing onomatopoeia of 'a short fierce fuse' (stanza four). The last three lines give us the huge ranging strides of the jaguar: each line is a new horizon.

SECOND GLANCE AT A JAGUAR.

Years later, the poet returns to the subject. (I have moved this poem forward in the chronological sequence for easier comparison with its predecessor.) Hughes has now largely abandoned regular stanzaic shapes; neatness and conventional expertise seem to matter far less to him. This poem is a series of artist's notes, not co-ordinated or formulated like the first jaguar poem. But the accuracy of the notes can hardly be disputed: there is a wealth of detail in the thirty-odd lines; and it is interesting to see how similar the tone remains. To Hughes such power is impressive, but also sinister: the images are of oriental ritual and physical aggression: the jaguar is a beast of 'the underworld'.

HAWK ROOSTING
Whether or not Hughes set out to write a poem merely about a hawk, he has certainly written more: a poem about a fanatic in power, about a natural evil (compare PIKE), about a hostile Creator? But it remains also a poem about a hawk, roosting: as such vivid and frightening. Much of the excellence of Hughes's 'symbolic' poems lies in their fidelity to 'the thing itself'; where many poets start with A, make it symbolize B, and are content, Hughes says 'A symbolizes B, which is powerfully represented by A'. The hawk, the pike, the thought-fox are *in themselves* engrossing and significant.

WIND
Again a phenomenon of the natural universe is terrifying, and breaks all routine and security. The violence of the wind is superbly presented in the verbs and participles of straining motion, the brutal surrealism of 'flexing like the lens of a mad eye', and the images of tension in the later verses.

11. *the brunt wind*: the full force of the wind.

SUNSTROKE
Mowing, the poet catches sunstroke, has terrible hallucinations and collapses. He is brought round in the gloom of the engine-shed, where the cool sunless stone and iron are welcome. Outside it is now raining. But all is not quite well: the last image is of the dead fox, appearing in its leap 'surprised by the rain'. It is a poem of remarkable terseness, a great deal compressed into a few tight pairs of lines.

NOVEMBER

In his descriptive writing Hughes constantly tries to get to the heart of things, to see their essential function or essential nature. Here, beside the vivid picture of rain, we are shown the thorn-roots with 'their grip on darkness', and the buried stones 'taking the weight of winter'. The tramp's life appears to be one of some 'strong trust' in the natural world, that it will allow him existence if he submits to it; but the poet uneasily notes, at the end, dead creatures strung up by a keeper, some of whom, in their death, seem to take a similar posture to that of the sleeping, trusting tramp.

YOU DRIVE IN A CIRCLE

'You' may mean 'I' (the poet), but is extended to include us all. We all try to evade something, like this or in some other way; and it is a useless attempt.

FULL MOON AND LITTLE FRIEDA

An example of Hughes's more recent manner: a more personal and fragmentary style, in free verse recalling that of D. H. Lawrence. The poem is an attempt to capture a moment, without interpreting it: in many ways a much more difficult venture than Hughes's earlier, more orthodox poems.

A WIND FLASHES THE GRASS

A recent poem, in freer verse and less coherent statement than the early Hughes poems, but with similar preoccupations: the mystery of the world, and its apparent malevolence. The added theme is the blankness of mortality: the ploughman senses his past and his ultimate future; the trees too are mortal—and the poem itself begins, at the end, to disintegrate, as 'shadow' seizes the poet's mind.

Seamus Heaney

Seamus Heaney was born in 1939 on a farm in Co. Derry, the eldest of eight children, three of whom still work on the farm. He, however, had an academic training and is now a lecturer in English at his old university, Queen's University, Belfast. His first book of poetry, *Death of a Naturalist*, was published in 1966, and is concerned principally with that farm background viewed in retrospect by the poet who has come to the city. Heaney is uncomfortably aware, in his own words, that he is 'the first of a line of farmers/dealers to have broken the hold of the home and the land' but that 'at the same time, the old traditional community which I knew as a child has disappeared'.

Heaney writes of these things calmly but sensitively. His own involvement does not exclude us: there are few private references, and the descriptive clarity of his writing makes it easy to follow. He uses words with something of the directness and onomatopoeia of Ted Hughes, whose work perhaps has influenced him. But Heaney's world is a warm, even optimistic one, by comparison with the sinister ferocity of Hughes: his tone is that of traditional sanity and humanity.

Digging

Between my finger and my thumb
The squat pen rests; snug as a gun.

Under my window, a clean rasping sound
When the spade sinks into gravelly ground;
My father, digging. I look down

Till his straining rump among the flowerbeds
Bends low, comes up twenty years away
Stooping in rhythm through potato drills
Where he was digging.

The coarse boot nestled on the lug, the shaft
Against the inside knee was levered firmly.
He rooted out tall tops, buried the bright edge deep
To scatter new potatoes that we picked
Loving their cool hardness in our hands.

By God, the old man could handle a spade.
Just like his old man.

My grandfather cut more turf in a day
Than any other man on Toner's bog.
Once I carried him milk in a bottle
Corked sloppily with paper. He straightened up
To drink, then fell to right away

Nicking and slicing neatly, heaving sods
Over his shoulder, going down and down
For the good turf. Digging.

The cold smell of potato mould, the squelch and slap
Of soggy peat, the curt cuts of an edge
Through living roots awaken in my head.
But I've no spade to follow men like them.

Between my finger and my thumb
The squat pen rests.
I'll dig with it.

Churning Day

A thick crust, coarse-grained as limestone rough-cast,
hardened gradually on top of the four crocks
that stood, large pottery bombs, in the small pantry.
After the hot brewery of gland, cud and udder
cool porous earthenware fermented the buttermilk
for churning day, when the hooped churn was scoured
with plumping kettles and the busy scrubber
echoed daintily on the seasoned wood.
It stood then, purified, on the flagged kitchen floor.

Out came the four crocks, spilled their heavy lip
of cream, their white insides, into the sterile churn.
The staff, like a great whisky muddler fashioned
in deal wood, was plunged in, the lid fitted.
My mother took first turn, set up rhythms
that slugged and thumped for hours. Arms ached.
Hands blistered. Cheeks and clothes were spattered
with flabby milk.

       Where finally gold flecks
began to dance. They poured hot water then,
sterilized a birchwood-bowl
and little corrugated butter-spades.
Their short stroke quickened, suddenly
a yellow curd was weighting the churned-up white,
heavy and rich, coagulated sunlight
that they fished, dripping, in a wide tin strainer,
heaped up like gilded gravel in the bowl.

The house would stink long after churning day,
acrid as a sulphur mine. The empty crocks
were ranged along the wall again, the butter
in soft printed slabs was piled on pantry shelves.
And in the house we moved with gravid ease,
our brains turned crystals full of clean deal churns,
the plash and gurgle of the sour-breathed milk,
the pat and slap of small spades on wet lumps.

The Barn

Threshed corn lay piled like grit of ivory
Or solid as cement in two-lugged sacks.
The musty dark hoarded an armoury
Of farmyard implements, harness, plough-socks.

The floor was mouse-grey, smooth, chilly concrete.
There were no windows, just two narrow shafts
Of gilded motes, crossing, from air-holes slit
High in each gable. The one door meant no draughts

All summer when the zinc burned like an oven.
A scythe's edge, a clean spade, a pitch-fork's prongs:
Slowly bright objects formed when you went in.
Then you felt cobwebs clogging up your lungs

And scuttled fast into the sunlit yard.
And into nights when bats were on the wing
Over the rafters of sleep, where bright eyes stared
From piles of grain in corners, fierce, unblinking.

The dark gulfed like a roof-space. I was chaff
To be pecked up when birds shot through the air-slits.
I lay face-down to shun the fear above.
The two-lugged sacks moved in like great blind rats.

Dawn Shoot

Clouds ran their wet mortar, plastered the daybreak
Grey. The stones clicked tartly
If we missed the sleepers but mostly
Silent we headed up the railway
Where now the only steam was funnelling from cows
Ditched on their rumps beyond hedges,
Cudding, watching, and knowing.
The rails scored a bull's-eye into the eye
Of a bridge. A corncrake challenged
Unexpectedly like a hoarse sentry
And a snipe rocketed away on reconnaissance.
Rubber-booted, belted, tense as two parachutists,
We climbed the iron gate and dropped
Into the meadow's six acres of broom, gorse and dew.

A sandy bank, reinforced with coiling roots,
Faced you, two hundred yards from the track.
Snug on our bellies behind a rise of dead whins,
Our ravenous eyes getting used to the greyness,
We settled, soon had the holes under cover.
This was the den they all would be heading for now,
Loping under ferns in dry drains, flashing
Brown orbits across ploughlands and grazing.

The plaster thinned at the skyline, the whitewash
Was bleaching on houses and stables,
The cock would be sounding reveille
In seconds.
And there was one breaking
In from the gap in the corner.

Donnelly's left hand came up
And came down on my barrel. This one was his.
'For Christ's sake,' I spat, 'Take your time, there'll be
    more.'
There was the playboy trotting up to the hole
By the ash tree, 'Wild rover no more,'
Said Donnelly and emptied two barrels
And got him. I finished him off.

Another snipe catapulted into the light,
A mare whinnied and shivered her haunches
Up on a hill. The others would not be back
After three shots like that. We dandered off
To the railway; the prices were small at that time
So we did not bother to cut out the tongue.
The ones that slipped back when the all clear got round
Would be first to examine him.

At a Potato Digging

I

A mechanical digger wrecks the drill,
Spins up a dark shower of roots and mould.
Labourers swarm in behind, stoop to fill
Wicker creels, fingers go dead in the cold.

Like crows attacking crow-black fields, they stretch
A higgledy line from hedge to headland;
Some pairs keep breaking ragged ranks to fetch
A full creel to the pit and straighten, stand

Tall for a moment but soon stumble back
To fish a new load from the crumbled surf.
Heads bow, trunks bend, hands fumble towards the black
Mother. Processional stooping through the turf

Recurs mindlessly as autumn. Centuries
Of fear and homage to the famine god
Toughen the muscles behind their humbled knees,
Make a seasonal altar of the sod.

II

Flint-white, purple. They lie scattered
like inflated pebbles. Native
to the black hutch of clay
where the halved seed shot and clotted
these knobbed and slit-eyed tubers seem
the petrified hearts of drills. Split
by the spade, they show white as cream.

Good smells exude from crumbled earth.
The rough bark of humus erupts
knots of potatoes (a clean birth)
whose solid feel, whose wet inside
promises taste of ground and root.
To be piled in pits; live skulls, blind-eyed.

III

Live skulls, blind-eyed, balanced on
wild higgledy skeletons
scoured the land in 'forty-five,
wolfed the blighted root and died.

The new potato, sound as stone,
putrefied when it had lain
three days in the long clay pit.
Millions rotted along with it.

Mouths tightened in, eyes died hard,
faces chilled to a plucked bird.
In a million wicker huts
beaks of famine snipped at guts.

A people hungering from birth,
grubbing, like plants, in the bitch earth,
were grated with a great sorrow.
Hope rotted like a marrow.

Stinking potatoes fouled the land,
pits turned pus into filthy mounds:
and where potato diggers are
you smell the running sore.

IV

Under a gay flotilla of gulls
The rhythm deadens, the workers stop.
Brown bread and tea in bright canfuls
Are served for lunch. Dead-beat, they flop

Down in the ditch and take their fill,
Thankfully breaking timeless fasts;
Then, stretched on the faithless ground, spill
Libations of cold tea, scatter crusts.

For the Commander of the 'Eliza'

... The others, with emaciated faces and prominent, staring eyeballs, were evidently in an advanced state of starvation. The officer reported to Sir James Dombrain ... and Sir James, 'very inconveniently', wrote Routh, 'interfered'.

CECIL WOODHAM-SMITH: *The Great Hunger*

Routine patrol off West Mayo; sighting
A rowboat heading unusually far
Beyond the creek, I tacked and hailed the crew
In Gaelic. Their stroke had clearly weakened
As they pulled to, from guilt or bashfulness
I was conjecturing when, O my sweet Christ,
We saw piled in the bottom of their craft
Six grown men with gaping mouths and eyes
Bursting the sockets like spring onions in drills.
Six wrecks of bone and pallid, tautened skin.
'Bia, bia,

Bia'. In whines and snarls their desperation
Rose and fell like a flock of starving gulls.
We'd known about the shortage but on board
They always kept us right with flour and beef
So understand my feelings, and the men's,
Who had no mandate to relieve distress
Since relief was then available in Westport—
Though clearly these poor brutes would never make it.
I had to refuse food: they cursed and howled
Like dogs that had been kicked hard in the privates.
When they drove at me with their starboard oar
(Risking capsize themselves) I saw they were
Violent and without hope. I hoisted
And cleared off. Less incidents the better.

Next day, like six bad smells, those living skulls
Drifted through the dark of bunks and hatches
And once in port I exorcised my ship
Reporting all to the Inspector General.
Sir James, I understand, urged free relief
For famine victims in the Westport Sector
And earned tart reprimand from good Whitehall.
Let natives prosper by their own exertions;
Who could not swim might go ahead and sink.
'The Coast Guard with their zeal and activity
Are too lavish' were the words, I think.

Follower

My father worked with a horse-plough,
His shoulders globed like a full sail strung
Between the shafts and the furrow.
The horses strained at his clicking tongue.

An expert. He would set the wing
And fit the bright steel-pointed sock.
The sod rolled over without breaking.
And the headrig, with a single pluck

Of reins, the sweating team turned round
And back into the land. His eye
Narrowed and angled at the ground,
Mapping the furrow exactly.

I stumbled in his hob-nailed wake,
Fell sometimes on the polished sod;
Sometimes he rode me on his back
Dipping and rising to his plod.

I wanted to grow up and plough,
To close one eye, stiffen my arm.
All I ever did was follow
In his broad shadow round the farm.

I was a nuisance, tripping, falling,
Yapping always. But today
It is my father who keeps stumbling
Behind me, and will not go away.

Mid-Term Break

[handwritten annotations: "life transitory" / "with life / in term / body"]

I sat all morning in the college sick bay
Counting bells knelling classes to a close.
At two o'clock our neighbours drove me home.

In the porch I met my father crying—
He had always taken funerals in his stride—
And Big Jim Evans saying it was a hard blow.

The baby cooed and laughed and rocked the pram
When I came in, and I was embarrassed
By old men standing up to shake my hand

And tell me they were 'sorry for my trouble'.
Whispers informed strangers I was the eldest,
Away at school, as my mother held my hand

In hers and coughed out angry tearless sighs.
At ten o'clock the ambulance arrived
With the corpse, stanched and bandaged by the nurses.

Next morning I went up into the room. Snowdrops
And candles soothed the bedside; I saw him
For the first time in six weeks. Paler now,

Wearing a poppy bruise on his left temple,
He lay in the four foot box as in his cot.
No gaudy scars, the bumper knocked him clear.

A four foot box, a foot for every year.

The Play Way

Sunlight pillars through glass, probes each desk
For milk-tops, drinking straws and old dry crusts.
The music strides to challenge it
Mixing memory and desire with chalk dust.

My lesson notes read: Teacher will play
Beethoven's Concerto Number Five
And class will express themselves freely
In writing. One said 'Can we jive?'

When I produced the record, but now
The big sound has silenced them. Higher
And firmer, each authoritative note
Pumps the classroom up tight as a tyre

Working its private spell behind eyes
That stare wide. They have forgotten me
For once. The pens are busy, the tongues mime
Their blundering embrace of the free

Word. A silence charged with sweetness
Breaks short on lost faces where I see
New looks. Then notes stretch taut as snares. They trip
To fall into themselves unknowingly.

Honeymoon Flight

Below, the patchwork earth, dark hems of hedge,
The long grey tapes of road that bind and loose
Villages and fields in casual marriage:
We bank above the small lough and farmhouse

And the sure green world goes topsy-turvy
As we climb out of our familiar landscape.
The engine noises change. You look at me.
The coastline slips away beneath the wing-tip.

And launched right off the earth by force of fire
We hang, miraculous, above the water,
Dependent on the invisible air
To keep us airborne and to bring us further.

Ahead of us the sky's a geyser now.
A calm voice talks of cloud yet we feel lost.
Air-pockets jolt our fears and down we go.
Travellers, at this point, can only trust.

May Day

The whole county apparently afloat:
Every road bridging or skirting water,
The land islanded, lough and burn turned moat.

That bulrush at attention. I had to
Wade barefoot over spongy, ice-cold marsh
(No bottom, just water seeping through

The netted weed) to get near where it stood
Perennially dry among May blossoming,
Chalky, velvety, rooted in liquid.

The elements running to watercolour,
The skyline filled up to the very brim.
The globe was flooded inwardly, fuller

Than a melon, the rind not even solid
For remember, in a ditch, the unstanched spring
Flushing itself all over the road.

Notes

DIGGING
The first poem in Seamus Heaney's first volume: the poet pledges himself to try to make poems with the same skill and perseverance his father and grandfather gave to digging. The poem also acts as self-introduction (compare Tony Connor's A RATHER PUBLIC STATEMENT)—Heaney wants us to know of his humble and Irish origins.

THE BARN
plough-socks: plough-shares.
gilded motes: specks of dust in a shaft of sunlight.

DAWN SHOOT
Heaney is a painterly poet: his visual descriptions are persuasive and show a painter's kind of observation. The first images here clearly suggest the texture of paint; later 'the rails scored a bull's eye into the eye/Of a bridge' shows an instinctive geometrical sense.
whins: gorse.

AT A POTATO DIGGING
drill: row of potatoes (the ridge of soil under which they lie).
creels: baskets.
I. Ireland has suffered 'Centuries/Of fear and homage to the famine god'. Potatoes have all too often been the main diet of her peasants. Today, even in mass gathering behind a machine, the poet feels a sense of reverence and ritual (the earth is 'the black/Mother').
II. A vivid picture of potatoes themselves.
III. A terrible description of famine in the 1840's, bitterly introduced by the use in its literal sense of a metaphor from the last line of II.

IV. Back to the modern potato-digging; the full significance of the occasion now clear to the reader. What is the point of the last two lines?

FOR THE COMMANDER OF THE 'ELIZA'
Another poem about the Famine in Ireland.

Make sure you understand and see the appropriateness of 'exorcised' in the last paragraph. The poem hinges round this word.

FOLLOWER
sock: the plough-share.

Compare DIGGING. The son's devotion to his father's memory is beautifully and neatly expressed; it is worth remembering, too, how the son feels he has broken away—perhaps ungratefully—from his parents' ways.

MID-TERM BREAK
The poet got a 'break' from boarding-school when his small brother was killed. The bewildered, embarrassed, numb feelings of the living boy are finely caught, especially in the inappropriate 'wit' of the last line.

THE PLAY WAY
The title is a half-ironic reference to modern educational theory. It seems as if the poet quite expected the music to fail (the bluntness of 'with chalk dust', the ironic note of a pupil's 'Can we jive?'): instead it works. The imagery of the poem, without being flashy, is immensely expressive and persuasive: 'strides' (line 3), 'Pumps the classroom up tight as a tyre' (line 12)—if you know Beethoven, and particularly this concerto, you will see exactly what is meant; the children's tongues wriggling around their lips as they write, seen by the poet as a mime of their discovery of the creative word; and, best of all, the last two lines: the music catches the children unaware, reveals parts of themselves they did not know about.

The flight, a climb 'out of our familiar landscape', acts as a symbol of the change in the life of the newly married pair. (Note the casual artistry with which, in the first lines, the image of marriage is introduced, from an unpromising routine 'patchwork earth', via 'hems' and 'tapes' to the bonds of marriage.)

The experience is a major one: and, as the third verse emphasizes, one in which the traditional four elements (earth, fire, water, air) all play a part. This is unexpectedly like seventeenth-century wit: the whole poem is in fact a piece of considerable ingenuity. The last line is beautifully ambiguous.

ACKNOWLEDGEMENTS

Acknowledgements are due to the following for permission to publish copyright material: Faber & Faber Ltd. for poems by Philip Larkin from *The North Ship* and *The Whitsun Weddings*; and The Marvell Press for 'Wedding-Wind' and 'Church-Going' from *The Less Deceived*; Wesleyan University Press for poems by Louis Simpson from *A Dream of Governors* and *At the End of the Open Road* ('The Goodnight' first appeared in *The New Yorker*); Louis Simpson for 'American Classic' and the *New Statesman* in which this poem first appeared; Oxford University Press for 'After Midnight' from *Selected Poems*; Charles Scribner's Sons, for 'As Birds are Fitted to the Boughs', 'The Battle' and 'Memories of a Lost War'; Oxford University Press for poems by Charles Tomlinson from *Seeing is Believing*, *A Peopled Landscape* and *American Scenes*; Oxford University Press for poems by Tony Connor from *With Love Somehow* and *Lodgers*; Faber & Faber Ltd. for poems by Ted Hughes from *Lupercal*, *The Hawk in the Rain* and *Wodwo*; Faber & Faber Ltd. for poems by Seamus Heaney from *Death of a Naturalist*; Seamus Heaney for 'May Day'.

In the case of certain poems by Ted Hughes, acknowledgements to include them in this collection for use in Canada are made to Harper & Row, Publishers, for 'Wind' copyright © 1956 by Ted Hughes, 'The Thought-Fox' copyright © 1957 by Ted Hughes and 'The Jaguar' copyright © 1957 by Ted Hughes (all from *The Hawk in the Rain*).